Living Faith

CP
Covenant Publications
CHICAGO • ILLINOIS

LIVING FAITH

Reflections on Covenant Affirmations

by the Faculty of
North Park
Theological Seminary

Edited by James K. Bruckner,
Michelle A. Clifton-Soderstrom, *and* Paul E. Koptak

Covenant Publications
8303 West Higgins Road, Chicago IL 60631

Copyright © 2010 Covenant Publications
All rights reserved.
Printed in the United States of America

20 19 18 17 16 15 14 13 12 11   7 6 5 4 3 2

ISBN 0-910452-97-0

All Scripture verses, unless otherwise noted, are from the New Revised Standard Version Bible, copyright © 1989 National Council of the Churches of Christ in the United States of America. Used by permission. All rights reserved.

Contents

FOREWORD vii

PREFACE xi

CHAPTER ONE
Common Christian Affirmations 1
Theological Reflection: John E. Phelan Jr.

CHAPTER TWO
The Centrality of the Word of God 23
Historical Roots: Philip J. Anderson
Theological Reflection: Klyne R. Snodgrass
  with Robert L. Hubbard Jr.

CHAPTER THREE
The Necessity of New Birth 49
Historical Roots: Philip J. Anderson
Theological Reflection: Stephen J. Chester, James Dekker,
  and Michael Van Horn

Contents

CHAPTER FOUR
A Commitment to the Whole Mission of the Church 73
Historical Roots: Philip J. Anderson
Theological Reflection: Michelle A. Clifton-Soderstrom,
    Paul H. DeNeui, and Soong-Chan Rah

CHAPTER FIVE
The Church as a Fellowship of Believers 97
Historical Roots: Philip J. Anderson
Theological Reflection: D. Brent Laytham

CHAPTER SIX
A Conscious Dependence on the Holy Spirit......... 127
Historical Roots: Philip J. Anderson
Theological Reflection: Richard W. Carlson

CHAPTER SEVEN
The Reality of Freedom in Christ................... 161
Historical Roots: Philip J. Anderson
Theological Reflection: Michelle A. Clifton-Soderstrom
    and Max J. Lee

FOR REFLECTION AND DISCUSSION 191

NORTH PARK THEOLOGICAL SEMINARY FACULTY 199

Foreword

The Covenant affirmations, the crisp description of the theological roots and convictions of the Evangelical Covenant Church, are uniquely important in articulating, nurturing, and transmitting the essential central identity of the Evangelical Covenant Church. Given the burgeoning growth of the church, it is timely to add to our array of resources that help us engage these formative principles.

This volume in no small measure is an elaborative commentary on the Covenant affirmations by the faculty of North Park Theological Seminary. That these same scholars love the church and are committed to its mission means this is no mere intellectual exercise. The book ultimately serves to call out the best in us for what it means to die to self and live instead with our hearts set on God. In the Covenant we want the focus to be on the clear, inexhaustible truths of new life in Christ around which we gather, not

Foreword

the periphery around which people tend to divide.

My anticipation for this book is captured in its title: *Living Faith*. Its double meaning pulls us into the two-step rhythm of being alive in Christ. When we understand "living" as an adjective, we are called beyond an intellectual acknowledgment of a set of theological propositions into an actual engagement of living with God. When we understand "living" as a verb, we are called to put what we believe into practice as we live for God. Living with God and for God is the simple, humble rhythm of the legacy that has been passed to us from generation to generation in the Evangelical Covenant Church.

While the Covenant Church has traceably lived these affirmations from its inception in 1885, it was not until 1976 that the Committee on Covenant Doctrine first framed them systematically (updated 2005). At that time President Milton Engebretson commented, "The Covenant Church is currently experiencing the joy of growth....We believe it is both right and the right of every person to know firsthand the basic beliefs favored by the denomination he or she belongs to." It is no less true of the rapidly growing mosaic of the Covenant Church today.

On behalf of the whole church, we extend thanks to those who have played such an important role in this project: project coordinator Mary Miller; faculty authors whose content is reflected in these pages; general editors Michelle Clifton-Soderstrom, Paul Koptak, and Jim Bruckner, who worked tirelessly to shape this volume; Donn Engebretson, who coordinated responses from a helpful cross-section of readers; and Jane Swanson-Nystrom for her always impeccable editorial expertise. A special note of thanks to the Lilly

Foreword

Endowment whose funding has supported this project.

Gary Walter
President, The Evangelical Covenant Church

Preface

What does the Evangelical Covenant Church believe? Ministers and members alike are asked that question, and it is typically answered by turning to a set of common affirmations that were written in 1976 and revised in 2005. While they were not intended to define doctrinal positions, the affirmations summarize a long history of biblical study and theological discernment. In so doing, they say something about the spirit of our common life. They demonstrate the way Covenanters have come together to discern the will of God and fulfill their calling as servants of the kingdom. The work continues today, and so the faculty of North Park Theological Seminary presents this collection of reflections to enrich the church's understanding of the tradition that guides its life and witness. The entire faculty participated in the conception, writing, and review of the chapters, so they present a model in miniature of what the Covenant Church has been doing throughout 125 years of its

Preface

global ministry.

The Evangelical Covenant Church falls in the line of believers' church traditions, and while we do not require adherence to particular doctrines for membership, we nevertheless cherish history and theology. In an attempt to cultivate theological reflection in the whole church, we identify six affirmations that shape our orthodoxy (beliefs about God) and our orthopraxy (lived faith). Affirmations are the significant theological guideposts for the Covenant. They are like doctrine in that they function as a theological reflection on Scripture, and we use them for teaching and instruction. Affirmations also extend beyond doctrine in that they function as beliefs that we actively affirm as well as seek to live out. For example, the first affirmation—the centrality of the word of God—points to belief in the authority of Scripture. However, just as importantly, affirming the centrality of the word means that we engage in disciplined practices that support our belief in Scripture's authority, such as reading Scripture together regularly. The affirmation of the church as a fellowship of believers points to the belief that God gathers the church and that the church is the communion of those who share new life in Christ. Affirming the church as a fellowship means that we befriend one another and are present to those people in our local fellowships. So, the Covenant's use of the term affirmation acknowledges the place of theological reflection, or doctrine, and extends our theology into corresponding practices that shape our life together.

This book is ordered according to the six affirmations of the Evangelical Covenant Church: the centrality of the word of God, the necessity of new birth, a commitment to the whole mission of the church, the church as a fellowship of believers, a conscious dependence on the Holy Spirit, and the reality of freedom in Christ. Each chapter has three parts: a historical introduction to the affirmation, the affirmation itself, and theological reflection on the affirmation. Each chapter is meant to inspire readers to engage the theological reflection in light of the actual affirmations and their historical context.

In reading through the chapters, one might note that they are not ordered according to when they were written; they embody, rather, a theological progression. The last affirmation, the reality of freedom in Christ, for example, does not make sense without remembering the first affirmation of the centrality of the word of God. The editors encourage readers to note the ways that the affirmations build on each other and reflect that the Christian life, and theology, emerges from a context.

With that in mind, we begin the book with a chapter on our common Christian affirmations, or those affirmations through which we connect with the whole of the Christian church. These four common affirmations—that we are an apostolic church, a catholic church, a Reformation church, and an evangelical church—frame the Covenant affirmations. These four common Christian affirmations offer the rich ecclesial environment in which the Covenant has been formed and with which it remains deeply connected. In addition, these four common Christian affirmations offer points of contact and reference for those persons reading this book who are either new to or unfamiliar with the Covenant. Situating the Covenant within the historical church is a key aspect of who we are and how we understand our distinctive six affirmations that follow.

Preface

The project was supported by the Making Connections Initiative (MCI) grant funded by the Lilly Endowment, Inc. Designed to bring the seminary into closer contact with churches, pastors, youth groups, and students of North Park University, MCI produced the original "Exploring Covenant Affirmations" video series and study guide in collaboration with the Department of Christian Formation. Special thanks goes to Mary Miller, director of MCI, who first conceived the idea of this book, convened our editorial committee, and coordinated a group of readers from across the denomination that included lay leaders, editors, ministers, and administrators. We are grateful to those readers for their encouraging and candid responses to the drafts; they helped us speak more clearly to the interests and concerns of the whole Covenant Church. In particular, Jane Swanson-Nystrom provided a wonderful editorial eye in the final stages, and this book is a better one because of her insights. We were greatly helped by the attentive work of Deidre Robinson, the counsel of Don Meyer, and the questions at the end of this volume written by Liz VerHage. Finally, we wish to thank Gary Walter, president of the Evangelical Covenant Church, for his enthusiastic support shown in many ways, especially in writing the foreword.

We, the faculty members of North Park Theological Seminary, wish to dedicate this work to our former colleague Michael Van Horn. Shortly after writing his piece for chapter three on baptism and new life, Michael was incapacitated by illness. His presence among us is greatly missed.

As one member of Christ's body the church, the seminary faculty offer these explorations of our theological self-understanding in anticipation that they will be read by those who are considering

Preface

joining the Covenant and those who have been Covenanters longer than they can remember. We hope they will be discussed, even debated, in small group gatherings and membership classes. Most important, we pray they will lead us to ever more faithful worship, testimony, and service.

JAMES K. BRUCKNER
Professor of Old Testament

MICHELLE A. CLIFTON-SODERSTROM
Associate Professor of Theology and Ethics

PAUL E. KOPTAK
Paul and Bernice Brandel Professor of Communication and Biblical Interpretation

1

Common Christian Affirmations

Covenanters unite around the theme of companionship. This idea is echoed throughout the chapters of this volume. Born of the Mission Friends and their commitment to sharing the gospel by cultivating relationships, the early Covenant Church hesitated to call itself a denomination because we are a people in communion with the whole Christian church. God has worked through the Covenant Church as a particular community of believers; however, we are woven into the fabric of God's larger salvific work throughout history. Given this understanding, it comes as no surprise that the Covenant affirmations begin by framing our beliefs and ecclesial identity through the lens of the whole church, and it is here—with our affirmations in common with the church universal—that this volume also begins.

We are an *apostolic* church. We confess Jesus Christ and the faith of the apostles as recorded in the Holy Scriptures. We believe the authority of the Bible is supreme in all matters of faith, doctrine, and conduct, and it is to be trusted. "Where is it written?" was and is the Covenant's touchstone of discussion with regard to faith and practice.

We are a *catholic* church. The word *catholic* literally means *universal*. This means we understand ourselves to be a part of the community of believers that began with Jesus's first followers, is alive today, and will continue until Christ comes again.

We are a *Reformation* church. We stand in the mainstream of a church renewal movement of the sixteenth century called the Protestant Reformation. Especially important is the belief that we are saved by God's grace alone, through faith alone, not by anything that we can do. The Covenant Church is also shaped by Pietism, a renewal movement that originated in seventeenth-century Europe and emphasized the need for a life that is personally connected to Jesus Christ, a reliance on the Holy Spirit, and a call to service in the world.

We are an *evangelical* church. A series of religious awakenings flowered in Europe and America during the nineteenth century and provided rich soil for the early growth of the Covenant Church with our passion for mission. Evangelicals historically have been characterized by a strong insistence on biblical authority, the absolute necessity of new birth, Christ's mandate to evangelize the world, the continuing need for education and formation in a Christian context, and a responsibility for benevolence and the advancement of social justice.

1

THEOLOGICAL REFLECTION

Christianity is complex. The three great divisions of the church—Orthodox, Roman Catholic, and Protestant—are only the beginning. Within Protestantism alone are thousands of separate denominations, as well-known as the Southern Baptists and the United Methodists, and as obscure as Two Seed in the Spirit Predestinarian Baptist.

Within this denominational complexity are theological cross-currents that muddy the waters further. Each tradition, for example, has its own form of "liberal" and "conservative" churches. Although all Christians share the same Bible, worship the same God, and follow the same Lord, Jesus Christ, they have very different views on the interpretation of that Bible, the character of that God, and the accomplishments of that Lord. They also have very different understandings of the mission, worship, leadership, and ministry of the church.

In addition to theological cross-currents there are ethnic, cultural, and gender cross-currents. The fastest growing part of the Christian church is south of the Equator. The church in Latin

America, Africa, and Asia is experiencing explosive growth. The black church in the United States is a powerful force not only in the African American community, but is increasingly influential in the wider church and culture. In recent years second-generation Asian churches have grown exponentially, especially within the evangelical community, and Hispanic churches have exploded in size and numbers. These churches are offering new vitality, new visions for mission and ministry, and new angles on the world for the white church.

The Evangelical Covenant Church grew rapidly through the 1990s and early 2000s. While it is still a relatively small denomination, it has a growing opportunity to impact this divided and complex church and society in North America. The Covenant affirmations give shape to its identity and mission. They provide a way to navigate the dangerous theological, social, and political crosscurrents that would swamp its mission.

The Evangelical Covenant Church did not come into being without antecedents. The affirmations are not without precedent. In the pages that follow those antecedents and precedents will be explored. Four declarative statements will guide this exploration:

- The Covenant Church is an apostolic church.
- The Covenant Church is a catholic church.
- The Covenant Church is a Reformation church.
- The Covenant Church is an evangelical church.

Although as a denomination the Evangelical Covenant Church did not come into existence until 1885, its history and identity are found in the work of God's Holy Spirit throughout the whole history of the church and indeed in the story of God's people Israel.

AN APOSTOLIC CHURCH

In Matthew 28, after the death and resurrection of Jesus, he called his now eleven disciples to Galilee. He gave them the following instructions: "Go therefore and make disciples of all nations, baptizing them in the name of the Father and of the Son and of the Holy Spirit, and teaching them to obey everything that I have commanded you" (vv. 19-20). In Acts 1 before he was taken into heaven Jesus told them, "You will be my witnesses in Jerusalem, in all Judea and Samaria, and to the ends of the earth" (v. 8). A bit later in Acts 2:42 we are told that the early Christians "devoted themselves to the apostles' teaching." These passages make it clear that the apostles are the *emissaries* of Jesus. They carry his message and mission to the world. Their teachings provided the core of the early church's identity and mission. Paul would tell the Gentile Christians in Ephesus that their community was part of the "household of God" that was "built upon the foundation of the apostles and prophets" (Ephesians 2:19-20). The church begins with the apostles' witness to Jesus.

In the New Testament there is a narrower and broader sense of the word *apostle*. Jesus appointed twelve apostles. After the betrayal of Judas, the small community of followers of Jesus added another apostle to take his place. Matthias was chosen for the role because he had "accompanied us during all the time that the Lord Jesus went in and out among us, beginning from the baptism of John until the day when he was taken up from us—one of these must become a witness with us of his resurrection" (Acts 1:21-22).

For the earliest Christian community an apostle, in this narrower sense, was a personal witness to the life, ministry, death, and resurrection of Jesus.

But a broader sense of the term emerged as the church grew and spread. Paul did not meet the criteria of Acts 1:21-22. But he still considered himself an apostle (see 1 Corinthians 9:1-2). Perhaps he was "the least of the apostles" but he was an apostle nonetheless—called by God to be a witness to the resurrection (1 Corinthians 15:9-11). Other men and even women (see Romans 16:7) would bear the title of apostle. Among them were Paul's colleagues Barnabas (Acts 14:14) and James the Lord's brother (Galatians 1:19). In this broader sense, apostle appears to refer to the earliest preachers of the life, death, and resurrection of Jesus and the founders of the earliest Christian communities. As far as Paul was concerned, his message was consistent with the original twelve and his authority no less than theirs (2 Corinthians 11:5).

Apostles in the narrower and broader senses of the term were the bearers of the message and mission of Jesus. They had heard Jesus's teachings. They bore witness to his resurrection. They formed his community. To be *apostolic* is to be faithful to the apostolic tradition, to the message and mission of those early Jesus followers as they were faithful to him. But those early apostles were going to die. What would become of their message and witness to the resurrection? In 2 Timothy an aging Paul tells his younger colleague, "What you have heard from me through many witnesses entrust to faithful people who will be able to teach others as well" (2:2). Paul knew that the time would come when the apostolic message would be forgotten or distorted if it were not faithfully taught and remembered (see 2 Timothy 4:1-5). The passing on of that *apostolic tradition* became one of the most important tasks of the apostles and their early disciples.

This was not done through verbal instruction alone, but, as in the case of Paul and Timothy, with written materials. The earliest existing Christian writings are the letters of Paul. Certainly stories of Jesus's miracles, teachings, and passion were circulating within the Christian community from its earliest days. But the four Gospels were not composed until the final decades of the first century. This written testimony was added to the memories of those who heard Jesus or the original apostles. In this manner the apostles' teaching was preserved and passed on.

But in the second century new teachers emerged to challenge the apostolic message. Marcion sought to eliminate the Jewish God and the Hebrew Scriptures and followed a truncated version of the Gospel of Luke and the letters of Paul. He argued the God of the Old Testament and the God of Jesus Christ were not the same god. The so-called Gnostics sought to eliminate or downplay the significance of Jesus's body. Some Gnostic teachers insisted Jesus did not really suffer and die. Some taught the physical universe was not created by God but by an inferior deity. These false teachers produced new gospels, new letters, and new apocalypses based on a very different theology than that of the apostles.

One response to these innovations was to clarify which writings were and were not faithful to the apostolic tradition. The word *canon* refers to a ruler or measuring stick. The canon of Scripture, then, is the list of books against which all other works and opinions must be measured. There were *four* Gospels, the early church

Common Christian Affirmations

insisted. The Old Testament was part of the Christian Scriptures. Paul's letters were in, but so were the letters of John, Peter, James, and other works like Hebrews and Revelation. But many other "Gnostic" gospels, letters, and other writings were not part of the canon of Scripture. The chief characteristic of a canonical book was that it was apostolic. This meant it was either written by an apostle, or a disciple of an apostle, or bore all the marks of the apostolic message.

A second response to the threat posed to the apostolic message was the development of Christian theology. Church leader Irenaeus of Lyon (c. 130-200) refuted the distortions of the apostolic message in his famous *Against Heresies*. He also wrote the *Demonstration of the Apostolic Preaching* by which he intended to preserve and promote what he understood to be the apostolic message. The second-century theologians included Justin Martyr, Theophilus of Antioch, Aristides, and others. Like Irenaeus they sought to refute the budding heresies of the second century through an appeal to the message of the apostles and the Scriptures. These reflections on the apostolic message and its encounter with pagan, Jewish, and heretical opinion formed the backbone of an emerging theological tradition.

Another way of preserving the apostolic message was the development of creeds. A creed is a concise statement of foundational beliefs. Many Covenant churches regularly recite the Apostle's Creed (see *The Covenant Hymnal: A Worshipbook*, #878). All Covenant pastors recite this creed at their ordination. While this creed does not go back to the original apostles, it was meant to preserve the key components of the apostles' teaching. It probably goes back to a baptismal formula used in Rome as early as the second century.

When Covenant people recite the Apostles' Creed or the Nicene Creed (see *The Covenant Hymnal: A Worshipbook*, #883), promulgated at the Council of Nicea (in 325), they are claiming continuity with those ancient Christians and all Christians who have sought to preserve, teach, and live by the apostles' doctrines. When Covenant people study the Bible and seek to apply its message to their lives, they are seeking to live from the apostles' teaching. When Covenant people bear witness to the resurrection and seek to make disciples, they are joining in the apostolic task. They are showing themselves to be part of an *apostolic* church, committed to the apostolic message and the apostolic mission.

A CATHOLIC CHURCH

The statement that we are a catholic church is confusing to some. The Covenant Church is a Protestant church. How could it be in any sense catholic? The word *catholic* means "the whole" or "the universal." To say that a church is a "catholic church" is to say it belongs to the "great church." Its identity is not confined to its local character or practices. However small and insignificant it may appear, it belongs to every other "catholic" church and every other "catholic" church belongs to it. Whatever God is doing in the world through his community, the church, the local church or denomination is part of it by virtue of being the Church of Jesus Christ.

The second-century martyr and bishop Ignatius of Antioch wrote to Christians in Smyrna, "Wherever Jesus Christ is, there is the catholic church." There is no thought here of the *Roman Catholic Church*. That is a later development. Rather, Ignatius has been warning about heretical teachers who are not faithful to the apostolic message about Jesus and who fail to care for the poor and suffering. When he says, "wherever Jesus Christ is," Ignatius means a *particular* Jesus Christ. He means the Jesus Christ of the apostles, not the "Jesus Christ" of the heretics. Wherever the "real" Jesus resides, the Jesus of the apostles, the Jesus of the gospels, *there* is the catholic church. For Ignatius the catholic church must also have leaders that are faithful to that apostolic message. A catholic church has Jesus Christ present and is led by apostolic leaders. A catholic church is faithful to the apostolic message. To be catholic is to be apostolic, and vice versa.

Cyril of Jerusalem (c. 315-382) would write,

> The church is called catholic because she is throughout the whole world, from one end of the earth to the other; because she teaches universally and without fail all the doctrines that ought to be preached to the knowledge of men concerning the visible and invisible, in heaven and on earth; because she subjects to her faith the whole of mankind—rulers and their subjects, educated and uneducated alike; because she is the universal physician and healer of sins of every kind, sins of soul or body, and possesses in herself every form of excellence that can be named in deeds and words in spiritual gifts of every kind.[1]

For Cyril, to be catholic is to make a universal claim for the gospel and for the church. It is to call the whole world to Christ's community, the church, for healing and salvation. It is to claim that the church is for the whole of creation on behalf of God.

The Evangelical Covenant Church is a catholic church in this sense. The Covenant Church is part of the one great thing God is doing in the world through God's community called the church. The Covenant Church is bold to claim that Jesus Christ is present with us when we preach and teach the word, baptize, break the bread and pour the cup, bear witness, and act with compassion. The Covenant Church is bold to claim that it possesses apostolic leaders who are prepared to teach and live out of the apostolic message. The Covenant Church is bold to claim that its mission is the mission of the apostles and prophets and of Jesus Christ himself. The Covenant Church is willing to cooperate with any other individual or community that is part of this great church, this catholic church.

By saying that the Covenant Church is a catholic church, another claim is being made. The Covenant Church is asserting that the whole of the history of the church is its history. Augustine belongs to the Covenant Church. So do St. Benedict, St. Francis, St. Clare, Julian of Norwich, and St. Brigid of Sweden. Martin Luther belongs to the Covenant Church. So do John Calvin, Huldrych Zwingli, and Martin Bucer. Philipp Jakob Spener belongs to the Covenant Church. So do Jonathan Edwards, John Wesley, and Billy Graham. Paul Peter Waldenström belongs to the Covenant Church. So do Martin Luther King Jr., Desmond Tutu, Mother Teresa, and Gustavo Gutiérrez. To say that the whole church belongs to us is not to say that we agree with or support everything it has done or said. It is not to say that the whole church has always been faithful to Christ or the gospel. It is not even to say that the Covenant

Church has always been faithful to the church or the gospel. It is rather to claim that wherever Jesus Christ has been working for the renewal of his creation, however faltering and fragile that effort may be, there is the church, the catholic church.

A REFORMATION CHURCH

The sixteenth century produced a religious, cultural, and political tsunami in Europe. The tightly woven tapestry of medieval Europe was already coming unraveled at the beginning of the sixteenth century. But few Europeans alive in 1500 could imagine the changes and cataclysms ahead. The most famous name of the Reformation era is, of course, that of the German monk Martin Luther. What began as a protest over the selling of indulgences, payments to escape purgatory, quickly spread to a wide-ranging critique of the theology and practices of the medieval Roman Catholic Church. Luther was more than an able polemicist, preacher, and writer. He was a Bible scholar. Tormented by the fear of an angry and judging God, Luther found in the Bible a very different way of understanding both God and human salvation. It is often argued that it was the publication of his famous ninety-five theses that launched the Reformation. But it could as easily be argued that Luther's study of the book of Romans really set the course of his life and gave shape to the Reformation.

The Roman Church argued that it was the church's tradition and the teaching authority of popes and councils that determined the meaning of the Scriptures and the nature of the faith. Luther argued that both the popes and the traditions were subject to error and that only an appeal to the plain meaning of the Scriptures would determine what was and was not apostolic. Luther found value in the theologians and teachers of the Christian past. He honored many of the traditions of the church. But it was God's word, not the word of any pope or council that should prevail in any argument.

Three phrases gave shape to Reformation theology: *sola fide* (faith alone), *sola gratia* (grace alone), and *sola scriptura* (Scripture alone). Luther found in Paul that a person was not justified on the basis of her or his good works. Rather, righteousness was the work of Christ. Luther insisted that the faith by which a person is justified is not merely intellectual or creedal acquiescence, but "a living, daring, confidence in God's grace so sure and certain that a man would stake his life on it a thousand times."[2] It was God in Christ that did all the work. And it was by *faith alone* that believers appropriated the results of that great work.

At the back of human faith was the *grace* of God. The initiative was God's. As Paul would put it, "in Christ God was reconciling the world to himself, not counting their trespasses against them" (2 Corinthians 5:19). This reconciliation was a gift of God—grace. "For by grace you have been saved through faith, and this is not your own doing; it is the gift of God—not the result of works, so that no one may boast" (Ephesians 2:8-9). God's salvation was pure gift. Nothing humans did could merit this gift.

All of this was made plain in the Bible. The Scriptures were not arcane documents accessible only to scholars and priests. They could be read and understood by anyone willing to read, pray, listen, and learn. As the sixteenth century wore on, Luther and his fellow reformers found that it was perhaps not as easy to interpret the Scriptures as they had originally thought. Significant differences between them emerged and divided the Protestant movement. Nevertheless, no one doubted that the faith was to be framed *by Scripture alone*. But how were the Scriptures to be read and interpreted?

Luther developed a dynamic way of reading the Bible. The written word was crucial to Luther. But even more important was the living Word, Jesus Christ. One read the Scriptures not simply for ideas, but to encounter the living Christ. The Bible was "the crib wherein Christ lieth." The living Word of God was present through the Spirit speaking through and empowering the written word of God. Scripture without the living Christ was only ink on a page.

Another critical aspect of Reformation thought was the "priesthood of all believers." Luther and other reformers denied that there was a special caste of individuals who were uniquely qualified to represent the people before God. This representative role was, in fact, the responsibility of all God's people. Peter wrote that believers were "a holy priesthood" offering "spiritual sacrifices acceptable to God through Jesus Christ" (1 Peter 2:5). For the reformers, all Christians were priests by virtue of their faith in Jesus Christ. All of them could represent God to the people and the people to God. All of them could read and understand the Scriptures and offer God worship and praise. This is not to say that the reformers thought the office of pastor or minister should be abolished. It rather meant that role was stripped of its exclusivity.

The Reformation spread quickly and attracted scholars and leaders from every corner of Europe. The major streams of the Protestant Reformation were the Lutheran, the Reformed, and the Anglican. The Lutheran movement began in Germany and spread to Scandinavia and elsewhere in northern Europe. The Reformed movement found its original impetus in Switzerland in the work of John Calvin, Huldrych Zwingli, and others. It spread through Eastern Europe, France, and the Netherlands and led to the development of Presbyterianism in England and Scotland. The Church of England was formed in the wake of the reforming movements of Europe and the marital crises of Henry VIII. Thomas Cranmer, the archbishop of Canterbury under Henry VIII, had been influenced by Lutheran thought. His reforming work led to his martyrdom under Henry's fiercely Roman Catholic daughter Mary.

Another major branch of the Reformation was the so-called Radical Reformation. These reformers sought to go back to the beginnings of the Christian movement. The most important group of this diverse movement was the so-called Anabaptists. The title refers to their rejection of infant baptism and their insistence on the baptism of adult believers. The word *anabaptist* means to "baptize again." There were many variations in Anabaptist thought, but all insisted on returning to the Scriptures for the pattern of Christian life and church order. Most were opposed to cooperation with the state and some were pacifist. Others were given to revolutionary violence. They were persecuted by both Protestants and Roman Catholics. They survive to this day in groups like the Mennonites. Contemporary Baptists are also heirs of the Radical Reformation although their history is more complicated.

The third branch of the Reformation is the so-called Catholic Reformation. In response to the growing threat of Protestantism, the Roman Catholic Church underwent its own process of reformation. The Council of Trent (1545-1563) dealt with the sort of clergy abuses that had led to the Reformation. It provided a rigorous and thorough statement of Catholic thought and set the pattern for clergy education and discipline. Many participants in the council hoped for a way to make peace with the Protestants by addressing the abuses they abhorred and clarifying and strengthening Catholic theological thought. The council framed the mostly fruitless conversations between Protestants and Roman Catholics for hundreds of years. It was not until the Second Vatican Council (1962-1965), convened by of Pope John XXIII (1881-1963), that new "windows were opened" for cooperation between Protestants, Roman Catholics, and Jews.

The Evangelical Covenant Church is clearly a Reformation Church. It affirms the three slogans: by faith alone, by grace alone, and by Scripture alone. It is also clearly a branch on the Lutheran family tree since it began as a movement in the Lutheran State Church of Sweden. But it has also been impacted by the Reformed family and the Anabaptist family.

The Covenant Church shares the Lutheran conviction that the Bible is a living document. One reads Scripture to encounter the living Christ through the Holy Spirit. The Bible is not merely a collection of theological propositions. The Covenant Church understands the Lord's Supper and baptism as sacraments of the church, as Lutherans do. God's grace is present in these acts of the church in a real and powerful way. But some Covenant people are more comfortable with the word *ordinance* to refer to baptism and the Lord's Supper. These are things done in response to the Lord's commands. Here the Anabaptist influence is felt.

The Covenant Church is firmly committed to the priesthood

of all believers. All God's people are gifted by God and called to represent God in the world as priests. This is a characteristic of the entire Reformation movement, although different branches express the "priesthood" in different ways.

Although the Covenant Church is clearly a Reformation church, it wants to remain open to fellowship and conversation with Roman Catholic and Orthodox Christians. It wants to keep in conversation with Protestant sisters and brothers with whom there may be significant differences. To be a Reformation church, a catholic church, and an apostolic church is to be committed to cooperating with every community of Christians where, as Ignatius put it so many years ago, Jesus Christ is present.

AN EVANGELICAL CHURCH

The word *evangelical* comes from the Greek word used to refer to the gospel. Luther and the other reformers believed they had rediscovered the gospel buried under the weight of traditionalism, hierarchy, and ignorance of the Scriptures. In that sense all of the churches of the Reformation were evangelical. The Evangelical Covenant Church is certainly evangelical in this sense. But over the years the meaning of the term *evangelical* has been shaped by cultural and theological forces that have impacted the Covenant Church as well as other denominations, churches, and individuals.

By the middle of the seventeenth century many European Protestants began to think the movement had gone awry. The vital living theology of the early reformers had become formal, rigid, and fierce. Mutual condemnations flew across the continent. Many of the controversies were trivial and created pointless acrimony and division. Other conflicts were more serious. Throughout the early part of the seventeenth century, violent wars devastated Europe. These conflicts pitted Protestants against Roman Catholics, as well as Protestants against Protestants and Catholics against Catholics. These conflicts disgusted many in the churches and academies of Europe.

The movement called "Pietism" arose in this context. Philipp Jakob Spener (1635-1705) was a Lutheran pastor who became a strong critic of what he saw as barren, theological rigidity in the Lutheran State Church in Germany. In 1675 he wrote an influential book entitled *Pia Desideria* or *Pious Desires*. He called for a faith in God that was less formal and more personal. He insisted that pastors and lay people make greater use of the Scriptures in their lives and ministries. He argued for a genuine commitment to the priesthood of all believers. Lay people, he thought, should have a wider role in the life of the congregation. He encouraged small groups of believers to gather together after worship services and at other times for the sake of mutual encouragement and learning. He wanted pastors to be prepared spiritually as well as academically. He wanted preaching to be straightforward and biblical. He argued for less theological wrangling between Christians who held many if not most important beliefs in common. Pietism's impact spread to other Lutheran countries, including Sweden.

A younger contemporary of Spener, August Hermann Francke (1663-1727) continued Spener's work. Francke established a center for Pietism at the University of Halle in Germany. He influenced Pietism through the development of schools, charitable work, missionary work, and the distribution of Bibles. Like Spener he emphasized the role of the laity, the importance of holy living, the centrality of the Scriptures, and the diminishment of theological wrangling. The immediate successors of Pietism were the Moravians, whose deeply mystical and personal piety led to the heart of John Wesley, the founder of the Methodist movement, being "strangely warmed." Wesley and the movement he founded had an enormous impact on the development of what became evangelicalism. In fact, a follower of Wesley, George Scott, brought a Pietistic revival to Sweden in the nineteenth century.

Today the evangelical movement is diverse, multidenominational, and multifaceted. But scholars of the movement argue for four enduring emphases:

1) The normative value of Scripture in Christian life
2) The necessity of conversion
3) The cruciality of the atoning work of Christ as the sole mediator between God and humanity
4) The imperative of evangelism

Missing in the list above but present in the early Pietists is the commitment to charity and compassion. This commitment shaped the Pietists in the seventeenth century, the Methodists in the eighteenth century, and the wider evangelical movement in the nineteenth century. It was evangelicals who started schools and orphanages, fought to abolish slavery, and sought to care for the poorest and most desperate in society. Only in the United States in the twentieth century did some evangelicals perceive a division between evangelism and social concern.

The immediate forebears of the Covenant Church were Pietistic Lutherans who were as critical of the Lutheran State Church in Sweden in the nineteenth century as Spener had been of the Lutheran State Church in Germany in the seventeenth century. They were looking for pastors and leaders whose hearts, like that of John Wesley, had been "strangely warmed." A formal relationship to the church was not enough. One needed a personal relationship with God through Christ. A passive engagement with the church was not enough. One needed an active involvement in worship, service, and witness. A life like everyone else's was not enough. One needed a holy life, a life that conformed to the Scriptures and the commands of Jesus. An individualistic life was not enough. One needed a communal life.

Our forebears learned from the Methodists to form small accountability groups for prayer, Bible study, service, and personal growth. These so-called "conventicles" were sources of accountability, learning, and mutual encouragement. Our forebears were committed to each other as they were committed to the gospel and the mission of the church. In fact they called themselves "Mission Friends," underscoring the very personal and communal nature of their commitment. They were friends and companions of all who feared God, regardless of denominational background. Anyone who followed Jesus was their friend in mission and worship.

The movement that became the Evangelical Covenant Church was part of what was called the "free church" movement in Europe. Free churches were those who in some sense broke from the state churches of Europe. There were (and are) many free churches in many countries. They developed their traditions, patterns of worship, and church organization over against a particular state church.

When the Swedes, Norwegians, and Danes who were part of Scandinavian Pietism came to the United States, they were free for the first time to form their own ways of worshiping and serving God without interference from the government or the state. The Pietistic Swedes who were our forebears also gathered for worship and witness. They founded churches throughout the East, Midwest, and West, and even a few churches in the South. In 1885 in Chicago they agreed to unify for mission and mutual encouragement. The Evangelical Covenant Church was born.

These early Covenant people shared the commitment of their sisters and brothers in Sweden to "the one thing needful"—a relationship with God through Jesus Christ. They were committed to the Holy Scriptures, the living word of God. They expected every believer to be "alive in Christ." These characteristics they shared with many people in the United States and Canada who had been impacted by the great revivals of the eighteenth and nineteenth centuries. But with the Pietists of the seventeenth century, they were opposed to theological hair-splitting and divisive controversies. They sought to cooperate with all who followed Jesus, even when they disagreed about important matters. They also demonstrated a commitment to the Pietist mission of caring for the poor and suffering. They were impacted by the rise of fundamentalism at the beginning of the twentieth century, but for the most part resisted its fierce separatism, biblicism, and legalism. The spirit of those seventeenth-century Pietists and nineteenth-century Mission Friends remains with the Evangelical Covenant Church to this day.

The Covenant Church is still committed to the living and powerful word of God. The Covenant Church is still committed to the necessity of conversion, to new life in Christ. The Covenant Church is still committed to mission and evangelism. The Covenant Church is still committed to a living faith and a holy life. The Covenant Church is still committed to compassion, mercy, and justice. *The Covenant Church is still an evangelical church, a reformation church, a catholic church, and an apostolic church.* In the pages that follow, the six affirmations of the Covenant Church will demonstrate how the church intends to remain faithful to its heritage and committed to its mission.

NOTES

1. Cyril of Jerusalem, *Catecheses* Lecture 18, Section 24.

2. Martin Luther, *Commentary on Romans* (Grand Rapids, MI: Kregel Publications, 2003), xvii.

FOR FURTHER READING

The Covenant Hymnal: A Worshipbook. Chicago: Covenant Publications, 1996.

Frisk, Donald C. *Covenant Affirmations: This We Believe.* Chicago: Covenant Publications, 1981.

Luther, Martin. *Luther's Small Catechism, with Explanation.* rev. ed. Moorehead, MN: Concordia College, 2005.

Spener, Philipp Jakob. *Pia Desideria.* Translated by Theodore G. Tappert. Philadelphia: Fortress Press, 1964.

Wilson, Everett L. and Donald Lindman. "What Does It Mean to Be Covenant? Covenant Distinctives." Chicago: Covenant Publications, 1988. www.vibrantpdx.com/our-vision-and-values.html

Waldenström, Paul Peter. *The Reconciliation: Who Was to Be Reconciled? God or Man? Or God and Man?* Chicago: John Martenson, 1888.

2

The Centrality of the Word of God

HISTORICAL ROOTS

The question "Where is it written?" continues to be the singular shorthand way of stressing the centrality of the Bible in the life of the people of the Evangelical Covenant Church through the generations. It is both a question that unites us and an expression of the desire to know that our beliefs are founded on the authority of Scripture, not on human explanations. Restated, "What do the Scriptures say?" this question is a compelling invitation to read the whole Bible thoughtfully and devotionally in mutual discernment and accountability. The question also leads Covenant people to understand God's word as the sole authority in a denomination that intentionally has not created its own creeds or confessions. The second article of the church's constitution contains its only confession: "The Evangelical Covenant Church confesses that the Holy Scripture, the Old and New Testament, is the word of God and the only perfect rule for faith, doctrine, and conduct."

The Centrality of the Word of God

The question, "What do the Scriptures say?" like all questions, comes from somewhere. It is historically rooted in a sustaining narrative and collective memory. The Covenant Church was conceived in the midst of a powerful grassroots movement of spiritual renewal in Sweden and among immigrants in North America during the nineteenth century. This movement, broadly known as Pietism, stressed personal conversion and the active living faith of persons transformed by the gospel. Its locus was in conventicles, small groups gathered in homes and elsewhere for prayer, worship, singing, encouragement, and Bible reading. Literacy rates were rising among peasant people and access to the printed words of Scripture, devotional writings, and songbooks meant that these Pietists became known among themselves and to others as *läsare*, that is, "readers."

It became natural, therefore, to rediscover in experiential ways the *sola scriptura* (Scripture alone) principle of the sixteenth-century Protestant reformers. There was an incredible hunger and thirst among these people, who often walked many miles simply to attend a conventicle, gatherings that remained illegal until 1858. The late Covenant historian Karl Olsson wrote: "You believed the Bible, you read it, you revered it; in it and through it God spoke his word of salvation to you.... You did not always seek to parse, to collate, to reconcile everything. You did not grub. You studied and you listened. That is the way it was."[1]

Paul Peter Waldenström, a pastor in the Church of Sweden and a leader of what would become the Covenant Church there in 1878, had gathered informally with a few colleagues during the summer of 1870. They were discussing the atoning work of Christ on the cross. One of them commented how wonderful it was that in the suffering and death of Jesus, God had punished him to the extent that fallen humanity deserved, in order that divine righteousness could be restored, wrath be appeased, and mercy be made available to the sinner. Another asked, "Where is that written?" Since it was an interpretation taught in the Augsburg Confession of the Lutheran State Church, they assumed it was everywhere in Scripture.

The question, however, did not leave Waldenström, and for the next two years he studied the Bible intently (he had a PhD from Uppsala University in classical languages), finally publishing a sermon on the question in 1872 arguing that the "penal subsitutionary" view was not that of the Bible or of the earliest Christians, but an interpretation developed much later within the medieval western church. Based on a close reading of biblical texts, his principal corrective was that in humanity's fall into sin, it was we who changed, not God. God's unchanging love, moreover, was the motive behind Christ's atoning sacrifice on the cross for the remission of sin, not an appeasement of wrath. God is not the object of the atonement but its subject. In this way, in the words of the ancient church, Christ in his voluntary and obedient identification with humanity became like us so that we might become like him. This sermon resulted in a storm of controversy that would help lead to the formation of the Covenant Church.

While Covenant people have been free to interpret Scripture regarding the doctrine of atonement, or any other, apart from definitive creeds and confessions, the guiding principle of the question "What do the Scriptures say?" continues to be an imperative call to test all things by a faithful reading of the text within the community of believers. Early Covenanters realized that this had become a defining moment in what would be the cohesive glue of a life movement in the witness of faith to each other and to the world. By claiming the Bible as its sole confession, these pioneers no doubt felt like a turtle emerging from its shell (how liberating yet potentially how vulnerable) or a sailor discarding the compass and the sextant for the ancient skill of sailing only by the stars.

In an address to Covenant pastors in 1898, North Park's first president, David Nyvall, said:

> Go to [the Bible] with an eye only for error and contradiction, grammatical anomalies, historical errors, mistaken data and numbers, and the Bible is big enough for a scholarship only of those things. But go to it with an eye for the life that billows forth in mighty waves in the water course, burst here and there, and you will be rewarded infinitely more. The Bible is a world that should be studied with a telescope rather than a microscope. What a loss it would be to study the stars or the northern lights with a magnifying glass.[2]

Interpreting Scripture is an act of worship of the One in whom we see ourselves as we really are, and it has always been at the heart of corporate worship in the Covenant Church—as in the words of an old Covenant hymn:

> For the hour of mercy granted
> we present our heartfelt praise;

The Centrality of the Word of God

thanks, O Lord, for truths implanted,
thanks for tokens of your grace.
Thanks for warnings, for instruction,
thanks for new born hope received;
thanks for light, blind fear's destruction,
for anxiety relieved.

Help us now your word to cherish,
sanctify our service Lord!
That your truth our souls may nourish,
be your will in us restored!
Help us in our daily living,
as we face the days ahead,
that we may be always giving
room to you, by you be led. Amen.

(David Nyvall, *The Covenant Hymnal: A Worshipbook*, #507)

2

THE AFFIRMATION

The Covenant Church states its view of Scripture as follows: "the Holy Scripture, the Old and the New Testament, is the word of God and the only perfect rule for faith, doctrine, and conduct."[3] When Philipp Jakob Spener presented his proposals for the renewal of the church in 1675, his first concern was with the centrality of the word of God in the life of the congregation and of individual believers. He wrote:

> Thought should be given to a more extensive use of the word of God among us. We know that by nature we have no good in us. If there is to be any good in us, it must be brought about by God. To this end the word of God is the powerful means, since faith must be enkindled through the gospel.... The more at home the word of God is among us, the more we shall bring about faith and its fruits.[4]

What was new in Spener's proposal was not another doctrine of inspiration (there was general agreement on the divine inspiration of Scripture in his day), or a new recognition of the authority of Scripture. What was new was his recovery of the living nature of the word of God. The word is the "powerful means" to the creation of new life through the Holy Spirit. For many in Spener's day the word of God was simply information, or law, or rules; for Spener the word was power—power to effect change in the life of the hearer through the Holy Spirit.

The dynamic life-shaping power of the word of God has been at the heart of the Covenant Church since its founding. That life-changing word gave birth to the conventicles—the small groups that met for Bible study in confidence that the word would shape the life of the believer and the believing community. It provided the motive for private devotional reading of the Bible, a practice for which our forebears received the nickname "readers." It prompted the concern for faithful preaching, not of human opinion, but of the word of God, which has power to convict of sin and unrighteousness and to kindle the desire for new life. This dynamic life-shaping power of the word leads us to affirm that both women and men are called to serve as ordained ministers. It is the reason we intentionally pursue ethnic diversity. It is the motivation behind every act of compassion and justice through the life of our shared ministry.

The Covenant Church believes that the effective power of the scriptural word is inseparably associated with the ministry of the Holy Spirit. The Spirit never works independently of the word, and the word is made effective through the Holy Spirit.

The union of word and Spirit is a central theme in evangelical faith. It was by the inspiration of the Holy Spirit that the written word came into being (2 Timothy 3:16). Through the Spirit the word of God does not return empty but accomplishes that for which it was sent (Isaiah 55:11). It is through the inner testimony of the Holy Spirit that the sinner who responds to the word is assured of being a child of God (Romans 8:16-17).

It is essential, then, to the life of the church that it be a company of people who desire their lives to be shaped by the powerful and living word of God. The alternative is clear. Not to be shaped by the word is to be shaped by the world.

On every side attractive and persuasive voices urge us toward conformity to the spirit of this age. There is no escaping from these pervasive influences. Only the church that hears and responds to the word will be able to be a prophetic voice in this wilderness and bring healing to a confused and troubled world.

2

THEOLOGICAL REFLECTION

The centrality of Scripture is the Covenant's heritage and its foundation. This conviction stems from a more fundamental conviction that God speaks, that is, God has spoken decisively in Jesus Christ and the Scriptures and God continues to speak by the Spirit through the Scriptures. The Christian church exists only because of this conviction. God is a communicative God, even if at the same time, as Isaiah 45:15 says, a hidden God.

The centrality of Scripture is the first of the Covenant affirmations and is asserted throughout the document because all the other affirmations stem directly from Scripture. Why so much focus on the centrality of Scripture? For the simple conviction that the Scriptures are the means to life because through the work of the Spirit they provide *access* to the living Word, Jesus Christ, and to God the Father, the giver of life. The word is central only because the God revealed in Jesus Christ is central to and foundational for all of life. The centrality of Scripture is really about the centrality of God, not just any god, but specifically the God revealed in Jesus Christ.

The Covenant has always asserted the centrality of Scripture, as indeed most Christians have. We believe it is central because it witnesses to a life, namely Christ's, and orders our lives. Toward this end, our focus is on Scripture as a *way*. Through it, we find the way to relate to Jesus Christ. This relationship to Christ through the living word takes precedence over all theories of inspiration. Theories of inspiration often are at bottom a quest for security, and we believe our security lies in God. People can say all the right things about Scripture and never have it function as central in their lives. Any claim to a commitment to the centrality of Scripture will not focus on words about Scripture but on performance with Scripture. A commitment to the centrality of Scripture gives regular attention to Scripture as the guiding and foundational principle for life, as the supreme authority that directs our thinking and conduct, and seeks thoughtfully to apply and live out the instruction of the text.

CONFESSING OUR FAITH IN THE CONTEXT OF SCRIPTURE

The Covenant does not require adherence to particular confessions, as some other ecclesial bodies do. Although we value the historic creeds highly, we confess them in the context of Scripture. This is why Scripture is so important. The ultimate authority and source for theology is neither creed nor confession but Scripture itself, because Scripture communicates to us the message from God. There we are told who God is, who we are, and the life God makes available to us. Especially without a fixed creed, Scripture and care in interpretation—hermeneutics—are crucial. Perhaps here is the place of the greatest failure of the church. We have affirmed Scripture without giving it attention, without treating it carefully on its own terms, and without heeding its instruction. We have talked

The Centrality of the Word of God

about the centrality of Scripture, but we have not shown people how to make Scripture central, how to understand it, and how to *live* the text.

The early Covenanters repeatedly asked the question, "Where is it written?" for they wanted to know that their beliefs and practices were in keeping with God's word. They sought a living faith, and the Bible was the most important means of achieving that. They knew that interpreting Scripture is an *act of worship* of the One in whom we see ourselves as we really are. The Bible is, as Covenanters have long recognized, an altar where we meet God, and reading Scripture has always been—and should be—at the heart of corporate worship in the Covenant Church.

If Scripture is where we meet God, it is not merely information about God. The phrase "the authority of Scripture" is not only a statement about the Bible, and the authority does not only reside in pages of paper and ink. The phrase "the authority of Scripture" points to the authority of *God*, the God revealed in and at work through Scripture. To say Scripture is central and authoritative is to use a *language of protest* that refuses to allow others to dictate how life is and should be. In the Reformation the protest was against the Catholic Church. In our day the protest must be against the dictates and idolatries of our society. Only God revealed in Jesus Christ has the authority, wisdom, and good will toward us to direct our lives.

In focusing on Jesus Christ, we do not in any way denigrate or devalue the Old Testament, as the heretic Marcion did. Quite the contrary, we affirm that all sixty-six books of the Bible are fully Scripture, with both testaments being equal partners in the canon. Both testaments inform worship and life for Christians today. There are wonderful teachings in the Old Testament, teachings about creation, the double love command so crucial for Jesus and the early church, the moral instruction of the law, the prophetic call for justice and expressions of hope, the praises and laments of the Psalms, and wisdom for life. Jesus and the first Christians assumed the teaching of the Old Testament was completely authoritative. The New Testament brings the Old Testament's larger narrative to its long-awaited completion in the message about Jesus the Christ. As Hebrews 1:1-2 indicates, God spoke in various ways in the past through the prophets, but God spoke decisively and climactically in his Son. The reality of God's revelation in Christ gives substance and meaning to the Old Testament story and becomes the key to understanding that earlier story. The teachings in the Old Testament take on new significance, especially in light of the cross and resurrection.

The relation of revelation, Scripture, and Christ as Word of God is important. Jesus is Word of God in a sense that Scripture is not. He is Word of God because he is the ultimate revelation of God and with the Spirit an agent of God's relation to the world. Revelation 19:13 even says his name is called "the Word of God." John 1:1-18 and Hebrews 1:1-4 also focus on Jesus Christ as the Word, the creator and ultimate revealer, and God's means of communication with us. We believe the Bible is God's word because it communicates to us the living Word, Jesus Christ. Yet, we cannot have the revelation in Christ without the written word. Apart from Scripture we do not know Jesus as the incarnate Word of God, the revealer, except in the most limited way, to take nothing away from creation as revelation. The text stands as Word of God, the access with the help of the Holy Spirit to the fundamental revelation in Jesus Christ.

THE ONLY PERFECT RULE FOR FAITH, DOCTRINE, AND CONDUCT

In Covenant thinking Scripture is central because it is the "only perfect rule for faith, doctrine, and conduct." Four times the Covenant affirmations use this statement, a statement that is easily misunderstood, especially if one thinks of problematic and violent passages in the Bible. The precise origin of the Covenant's statement is unclear, but surely it is an extension of the Reformation principle of *sola scriptura* (Scripture alone) and is close to the intent of statements from other groups.[5] Already at the Covenant's organization in 1885 the "Rules for the Swedish Evangelical Mission Covenant" list first the name of the organization and second the confession, which is one sentence: "The Covenant confesses God's word, the Holy Scripture of the Old and New Testament, as the only perfect rule for faith, doctrine, and conduct."[6] "Conduct" might more appropriately be translated "life."

With "rule" the reference is to a guide, the gauge by which one measures what ought to be. The word *rule* had been used historically of Scripture and creed and even of ministry. By "perfect" the intent is to say "complete" in the sense of everything needed, what God intended. One does not need to go somewhere else to find what is needed for life. It is the rule to which nothing else is to be added—not that helpful information appears nowhere else, but that there is no other information *necessary* for relation with God and for living in relation with God. With "only" obviously the intent is to say that there is no other communication that functions on this level. However, *sola scriptura* does not mean we use only the Bible. No one does. It means, as theologians have long argued, that Scripture is the "norming norm" (*norma normans*), the standard by which all else is measured. Scripture alone is the standard by which we measure how closely our faith, doctrine, and conduct compare to what God desires. All thoughts about God and life are understood and evaluated by their conformity to Scripture. What we need for our relation with God, what we need to direct our thinking about God and the world, and what we need to order life is determined there. No other template can do the job or is needed in addition. Yes, difficult texts are there, but no other template is needed. To say that Scripture is the only perfect rule for faith, doctrine, and conduct is to say that Scripture is the organizing principle we use to direct our thought and living, the final *authority* in all matters of faith and life by which all else is assessed.

The Bible certainly does not tell us everything we need to know, but it sets the boundaries and the perimeter within which we are to live, grow, analyze, learn, think, and act. Scripture answers life's ultimate questions, such as: Is the world a creation or an accident? Is there a God or are we alone? Does God care? Are other people similar to us? How are we to live in relation to God and each other? Will we be held responsible for what we do? Why are we here? Do we matter? Is there hope? Take away Scripture and how does one answer any of these questions? Science does not have the answers, Hollywood does not have the answers, Wall Street does not have the answers, Washington does not have the answers, nor does anyone else. Without Scripture and the God who authored it, why be ethical? The problem is that our churches and our society want to take the frame of Scripture, assume it as an overarching scheme, but not take it in substance and form that in any way actually is central and actually informs and directs life.

The answers to such questions come in terms of the loving, merciful God who is revealed in Jesus Christ, who seeks truth and justice, and in that respect Scripture gives us what we need for life: truth, justice, love, mercy, compassion, and hope. In the process it teaches us how to deal with our own egos, the source of sin. Scripture is the only perfect rule because it tells us who God is and who we are, what God has done and will do and what we should do. It gives us the materials to shape our identity in a positive and hopeful direction, regardless of what else is true of us. As Christians we are asked to take our identity from our God and from someone else's story, the story of Christ, and especially his death and resurrection. The Bible is an identity-shaping document. It is counter-cultural, refusing to accept the identity this society seeks to give us in favor of being who God says we are.

The issue is always, what does the text tell us about the identity of God and about our own identity. To say Scripture is central is to say that this collection of ancient books determines our identity. It tells us who we are before God and what we are to do, not just generally, but daily as we live our lives, how we are to understand this world in which we live, what to do when we and others fail, and how we are to live in relation to others, whether they agree with us or not. The text tells us who we are, where we belong, how we fit in God's story, in what God is doing, what we are to do, and where we are going. As one person put it, we decipher life in the mirror of the text. We are asked to place ourselves in God's ongoing story with Israel, Jesus, and the church, and to live from that narrative. All is part of a larger story.

Consequently, Scripture shows us what error looks like and what its consequences are. It shows us what a human is to be by showing us the face of Jesus Christ. It shows us who God is in that same face. It shows us that God has a purpose, is faithful, and will fulfill God's promise. It gives us value and good work to do and takes us beyond the silliness and meaninglessness of human existence without God. It confronts the evil in us and the evil and violence and injustice in this world and calls us out of that pattern. If this sounds too personal and self-centered, it is; otherwise it has no effect. But, by focusing on our true self, the Scripture as the voice of God calls us out of our self-centeredness, and it also teaches us how to praise and thus to find wholeness outside ourselves.

Scripture is central for other reasons as well. Scripture is central because the Spirit uses Scripture to transform our being. We seek transformational reading, knowing well that we need transformation. In John 6:63 Jesus says his words are Spirit and life, meaning "they are life-giving Spirit." The Bible is *the source, pattern, and power* (or catalyst) of truth, the foundation for existence in that it communicates the One who is life. It is the source of truth because it tells us about true realities and events and about the true character of God. It is also the pattern of truth because it shows us what truth and error look like, the one to be imitated and the other avoided. The Scriptures are the power of truth because of the Spirit's work through the Scriptures to effect truth in human lives.

We must ask ourselves what script we are following. Everyone

The Centrality of the Word of God

has a script he or she follows, whether from parents, the society, or one people write themselves, plagiarizing from others. Should we trust the author of the script we follow? Is the script that is central to our lives God's word or some substitute?

A focus on the centrality of Scripture may sound simplistic, but it is not. This is a complicated world, and, yes, some unjustly use the Bible to avoid the complexity of life. In reality the Bible, if given fair treatment, forces us to deal with the complexity of life. The word itself is by no means simple and does not give simplistic answers.

Still, believing in the centrality of Scripture is not enough. Many over the centuries have believed in the centrality of Scripture and ended up with unorthodox beliefs and actions. A polygamist sect can claim the centrality of Scripture. Certainly Scripture is not something that can be applied mechanically or formulaically. We need a hermeneutical anchor and guide to take us in the right direction. For Luther it was what drives Christ. For others the guide was the rule of faith, the creed derived from the Scriptures. The Covenant resource paper "The Evangelical Covenant Church and the Bible" points out that the Covenant reads Scripture according to certain guidelines: *faithfully, communally, rigorously, charitably, holistically*, and with essential commitments to *grace, transformation,* and *mission*. These are trustworthy guidelines, each of them deriving ultimately from Scripture itself. Together they show that we need to be wise in working out our theology, what salvation means, and what the implications are for life.

Some texts are difficult or problematic, and the church needs much greater skill in handling its Scripture. There is a constant interplay between understanding texts, thinking theologically, and understanding how we interpret texts so that our later readings are better informed than our earlier ones. Theological and exegetical conclusions often drive us back to adjust our hermeneutic for the next step.

The guidelines by which the Covenant reads Scripture and the skill required set the direction both for seminary instruction and the life of churches. North Park Theological Seminary, the Covenant's seminary, requires those in the Master of Divinity degree program, the degree assumed for those ordained to word and sacrament, to study both Hebrew and Greek so that careful attention can be given to the concerns of the text and to the best resources on the text. At the same time, interpretation is not given over to the experts. Our emphasis on the priesthood of the believers requires the engagement of all Christians in reading the Bible together. We read communally, knowing that even those who are the most well informed need the community to understand the text just as the community needs them. This interplay of leaders and people assumes a focus on a communal reading of Scripture and on conversation about Scripture. Without such communal focus we cannot claim the Scripture is central.

Also, no particular theory of inspiration is assumed in the Covenant as *the* theory for either seminary or churches. As indicated earlier, no theory does justice to the varied character of scriptural writings. Crucial and not negotiable either for the Covenant Church or the seminary faculty are the truth and authority of Scripture and the attention that must be given to it. All of our convictions about life and community are grounded there.

The Centrality of the Word of God

MORE THAN BIBLICAL

We have no higher authority than Scripture, but being biblical is not enough. One can be wrongly biblical, and the church often has been, as is evident in the history of slavery or how people have understood human authority. We have read Scripture in ways that allowed us to control the message rather than hear it and be transformed by it. We cannot claim to believe in the centrality of Scripture and surreptitiously seek to control it. We seek to control Scripture when we read it selectively, reading only the texts we like, texts we consider safe and that will not bother our lives. We control Scripture by our hardness of heart and lack of vulnerability to the text. Instead of controlling Scripture, we need instead to place ourselves under the control of the Spirit and under God's word rigorously understood. To affirm the centrality of Scripture is to assert that Scripture controls us, not vice versa.

Nor is claiming to believe the centrality of Scripture enough. Scripture rarely functions as central in our modern society. Scripture is central only when it is given consistent attention in community, studied in community, and lived out in community. Surveys show that churches do not challenge people sufficiently and do not teach them Scripture in an adequate way. People both want and need to focus on Scripture, for the Bible is the most powerful catalyst for spiritual growth. The Old Testament urged people to tie portions of Scripture on their arms and foreheads as reminders that Scripture was to direct both their actions and their thinking (see Exodus 13:9, 16; Deuteronomy 6:8-9; 11:18-21). These people knew that Scripture should be central. We would not argue for literal observance of this practice, but we must find compelling ways to make Scripture central in what takes our attention, forms our thought, and directs our action. That Scripture portions were tied both on the head and the arm is instructive. Too frequently we are guilty of separating thinking from acting, as if merely thinking correct thoughts or having the right theology is sufficient. Thought and action in the end are inseparable, and what we really think will be lived. This too was a focus of early Covenanters who insisted on faith being lived.

READING IN RELATION TO ALL OF SCRIPTURE

To say all of Scripture is central is not to say it is all equal in relevance or value. None of us treats all of Scripture as if it were. Scripture is like a variegated quilt; it is multilayered with texture and must be respected as such. People have problems with Scripture precisely at this point: they do not realize how varied and multipurpose Scripture is. Some parts of Scripture must legitimately be given preference. A priority is rightly placed on the New Testament, which does not denigrate the Old Testament but does direct its reading. Some parts of Scripture are less directly relevant because they belonged with earlier parts of the story, which now have climaxed in the story of Jesus. All of the text is for us, but it is not for us in the same way. We read all texts in relation to the rest of Scripture and the story of God's actions. The church has always focused on certain parts: for example the New Testament focuses primarily on Genesis, Exodus, Deuteronomy, Psalms, Isaiah, and certain other passages such as the promises in Zechariah, Daniel 7, and Jeremiah 31. Many other texts are never discussed in the New Testament. That does not mean those texts are unimportant, but they are placed in a different relation to the larger story.

Not all of Scripture is about how life should be. Much of the Bible, particularly some problematic texts, is about how life was and is. These difficult texts are sometimes not as problematic as we make them, if we do justice to the whole of Scripture. The issue, the goal, is always the divine intent for humanity. The guidelines for reading Scripture given in the Covenant resource paper (as outlined earlier) prevent both reading passages in isolation and reading literalistically. We can read harsh texts within the context of the whole of Scripture and know that humans should not practice genocide or slaughter their enemies. Jesus used a prophetic-love hermeneutic, a focus on the prophetic message and the command to love God and neighbor, and if we do as well, we will read the whole of Scripture to understand the character of God and know how to sort out the divine intent for humanity.

Individual statements in Scripture are not the word of God by themselves. Each text, even the seemingly clearest, depends on the whole of Scripture for its understanding. We are accustomed to think of specific passages, especially our favorite texts, as the word of God, but each specific text belongs in a longer book, in the narrative of what God has done with Israel and Jesus, and in the larger canon, the whole, of Scripture. We need the whole text to understand the individual parts. The individual texts are the word of God only because of their role in the rest of Scripture. It is the whole of Scripture, not the parts by themselves, that is word of God. We cannot have the parts we like without all the other parts taking their rightful place in the story of God.

Faithfulness to the whole text is required. This means we also read parts we know are less direct and learn from them. Collectively we watch how we read and consciously work out a hermeneutic and theology as to why we read and apply the text as we do. Difficult texts should receive more, not less, attention. Without doubt, we are selective, but we need also to be fair, to be hermeneutically and theologically informed by Scripture itself.

A TRAJECTORY OF REVELATION

The centrality of Scripture also requires recognition that there is a trajectory of revelation that must direct our hermeneutic. Scripture has a narrative movement and direction and a progress, even a growth, of doctrine. Such a trajectory is obvious with the sacrificial system in the Old Testament and the cessation of sacrifice at some time after the cross and Pentecost. The way the Old Testament mandated treatment of slaves was a movement away from how they were treated in the ancient world, and the New Testament taught a still different treatment and attitude toward slaves and set a direction that later changed the whole notion of slavery. The biblical understanding of God involves a movement along a trajectory past the Bible itself to the church's conclusions about the Trinity. The Covenant sees the ministry of women also as a movement along a trajectory, one begun in the Old Testament with people like Deborah the judge and Huldah the prophet and escalated in major fashion by the ministries of women in the New Testament. We read holistically to understand the directions the Scripture is moving. Reading holistically does not permit jettisoning earlier texts; it requires understanding all the text together and allowing one text to help interpret or contextualize others. Further, a focus on the centrality of Scripture does not permit a trajectory to be created that ignores or sets aside explicit texts.

From all this it is clear that it is a challenging task to be biblical, and that we must exercise care as we approach the text. Parts of Scripture are difficult, puzzling, or distressing. Often various themes stand in tension, such as grace and responsibility, divine sovereignty and human free will, or faith and works. Our task as church communities, as readers, is to do justice to all the text, to be willing to hear the text, to read communally, and to be formed by Scripture so that we live out its instruction. Being biblical may be difficult, but it is not overly problematic. The text is quite understandable. As often noted, the problem with Scripture is not what we do not understand, but what we do understand and fail to live.

THE CHALLENGE OF THE CENTRALITY OF SCRIPTURE

How can we do justice to the centrality of Scripture? If we claim the word is central, we will give time to corporate and private readings of Scripture and will not settle for study of Scripture that is superficial and inept. Centrality has to do with time, attention, and defining power (authority) being given to Scripture. It grows from the conviction that the Bible is a book of life (John 6:63), the very sustenance by which we live. One metaphor Scripture uses to describe engagement with Scripture as sustenance for life is "eating the word of God." The only reason to ingest Scripture is because in the process you ingest the Triune God, the source and sustenance of every aspect of life. The psalmist says, "O taste and see that the LORD is good" (Psalm 34:8). People need more than physical food, and Scripture is the means to the necessary food for life with God.

The Centrality of the Word of God

We live by every word that proceeds from the mouth of God, as Deuteronomy 8:3 tells us. Another metaphor is hearing from the heart, which means we not only give attention to Scripture but we take it into the depths of our being and obey it. To believe in the centrality of Scripture is to live it, which has always been a conviction of Covenanters, and it is the challenge we accept.

NOTES

1. Karl A. Olsson, *By One Spirit* (Chicago: Covenant Press, 1962), 532.

2. David Nyvall, *Minneapolis Veckoblad*, September 27, 1898, 3.

3. From the Preamble to the Constitution and Bylaws of the Evangelical Covenant Church.

4. Philipp Jakob Spener, *Pia Desideria*, trans. and ed. Theodore G. Tappert (Philadelphia: Fortress Press, 1964), 87.

5. See, for example, the Genevan Confession of 1536 in J. K. Reid, ed. *Calvin: Theological Treatises* (Philadelphia: Westminster Press, 1954), 26, and The Epitome of the Formula of Concord in Theodore G. Tappert, ed. *The Book of Concord: the Confessions of the Evangelical Lutheran Church* (Minneapolis: Fortress, 1954), 464.

6. See Glenn P. Anderson, ed., *Covenant Roots: Sources and Affirmations* (Chicago: Covenant Press, 1980), 11.

FOR FURTHER READING

A Covenant Resource Paper: The Evangelical Covenant Church and the Bible. Chicago: Evangelical Covenant Church, 2008. Available at http://www.covchurch.org/resource/covenant-resource-paper-the-covenant-church-and-the-bible

Frisk, Donald C. "Revelation and the Word of God." Chap. 2 in *Covenant Affirmations: This We Believe.* Chicago: Covenant Press, 1981.

Gorman, Michael J., ed. *Scripture: An Ecumenical Introduction to the Bible and Its Interpretation.* Peabody: Hendrickson, 2005.

Marshall, I. Howard. *Biblical Inspiration*. Grand Rapids: Eerdmans, 1983.

Peterson, Eugene. *Eat This Book*. Grand Rapids: Eerdmans, 2006.

Wright, N. T. *The Last Word: Beyond the Bible Wars to a New Understanding of the Authority of Scripture*. New York: Harper San Francisco, 2005.

3

The Necessity of New Birth

HISTORICAL ROOTS

"Jesus stands outside the door—why not bid him enter? Though your weight of sin be sore, he can life and strength restore: hear his voice so tender. Troubled soul, I do implore, will you let him enter?" (*The Covenant Hymnal: A Worshipbook*, #327). These lines were penned by an anonymous Swedish hymn writer. A hallmark of Covenant life and spirit through the generations has been a natural inclination to ask questions of one another, whether standing in relationship or desiring friendship in Christ. While some have assumed the role of making declarative speeches to others about their spiritual condition and need of conversion, a simple question like "Are you a believer?" has been an invitation to a more authentic sharing of each other's journeys along life's common and often difficult pathway. Its character honors the mystery of God's regenerative initiative and work in the particularity of a human person, and echoes what Jesus said to Nicodemus about the necessity of being born anew from above. For some, the crisis of the soul culminates in a dramatic moment of decision; for others, a variety of experiences—often subtle and known only in hindsight—give witness to God's gracious transforming action of conversion. The Covenant Church embraces this mystery, and acknowledges that the human response of repentance and commitment to a new way of life is a testimony to what a loving God has already been doing and will continue to accomplish.

Carl August Björk (1837-1916) was a cobbler. A big man with a formidable personality, he proved to be a natural and respected leader. Apprenticed to a shoemaker at age eleven, by twenty he was a demanding master with four young apprentices in his employ. At nineteen he had joined the army and learned the rough and tumbled ways of life in the world. He played a mean fiddle at the Saturday night dances in his little community in southern Sweden, where alcohol flowed freely during an era of devastating societal intemperance. There was a group of Mission Friends that also gathered each Saturday evening for prayer and Bible reading. An elderly tailor in the community sought to befriend the young cobbler and often asked him questions about his life. This was in 1862 and Björk was twenty-five. Finally, after repeated invitations to attend a mission meeting at the schoolhouse, the little tailor confronted Björk: "You're afraid to come!" Even if curious, this had now become a challenge Björk could not resist. "Me afraid?" he said, "I am twice the size of you!"

So Björk came to the crowded meeting prepared to fight and argue; instead, he was courteously ignored all evening. His anger and frustration grew as he stewed in protest while the others quietly departed. In a unique kind of folk psychology, the old tailor reached up to pat the angry young man on the shoulder and said, "Poor little Björk. Poor little Björk," and he too went home. The Spirit had been mysteriously at work in the cobbler, for that evening in the quiet solitude of his room he relinquished his life to Christ.

This story of yet another Saul becoming another Paul is not an uncommon one throughout the history of the Christian church. The next Saturday, Björk gathered again with the Mission Friends and persuasively implored his friends to accompany him. A revival soon broke out in this small community, especially among the young. Two years later in 1864, at the age of twenty-seven, Björk emigrated to the United States and soon received a new calling, one he had not been seeking. Within four years he was pastor of the earliest congregation formed in the Covenant Church (Swede Bend, Iowa); he became the leader of the Mission Synod a decade later; and in 1885 he became the first president of the newly formed denomination, serving until his retirement in 1910. Though his pastoral leadership was distinctive, his conversion and the promptings that led to it fit a common pattern in the renewal movement. It also reveals something important about the experience of new birth and its character within the Covenant Church.

While there are many different kinds of personal narratives of conversion and the ways in which faith would grow in discipleship and service, an important source of popular literature is the songs written and sung, which consistently invite reflection, conversation, and moments of commitment and resolve. They were not only witnesses of the believing community but served the purpose of proclaiming the gospel and inviting others to new life in Christ.

The Necessity of New Birth

In them, one does not find words of condemning judgment, of "hell, fire, and brimstone." One is not led to fear the wrath of an angry God. Rather, the images depict a loving parent who is tender and gracious in wooing, patient and persistent in waiting for the prodigal to return home, or a shepherd who seeks the lost—a savior, friend, and brother. These are also relational images, where God's divine initiative is channeled through faithful followers who witness with their lives by coming alongside the other with patience and persistent urgency. The hymns and spiritual songs of the Covenant's heritage illustrate beautifully the use of the interrogative, that is, the questions that in many forms embody the simple one, "Are you a believer?"

Among the many examples, Andrew L. Skoog wrote, "O that Pearl of great price! Have you found it? Is the Savior supreme in your love? O consider it well, [when] you answer, as you hope for a welcome above.... O then answer these questions so pressing, before God, [lest] time's favor shall cease. Is the Pearl of great price yours forever? Have you Jesus, and in him your peace?" (*The Covenant Hymnal* [1973], #294). Employing the analogy of nature, Lina Sandell directed her question to the young whose lives unfolded before them: "In the springtime fair but mortal, in the day of fragile flow'rs, Christ is waiting at your portal, faithful through the passing hours. Though at every moment near you, is the Lord unheeded still? For how long will he continue speaking to your shuttered will? Open now, before the autumn sweeps the summer flow'rs away; open while the sun is shining—all to brief our earthly day!" (*The Covenant Hymnal: A Worshipbook*, #340).

Covenant people understand the new birth from above to be a

52

necessity. In it we become by grace radically transformed creatures in new relationships with God, one another, and all of creation. It grows and matures in the grateful life of obedience and in whatever way the personal gesture of invitation to a shared life in the kingdom of God may be extended.

> Do you live the life that's given
> through your faith in Christ, the Lord?
> Is your name inscribed in heaven,
> in the kingdom of our Lord?
> Do you live the life that's new? Tell me true.
> Do you live the life that's new? Tell me true.
>
> Pray that Jesus may awaken Spirit life forever new!
> Pray that sin may be forsaken,
> which breeds only death in you!
> Ask yourself each day he gives, "Do I live?"
> Ask yourself each day he gives, "Do I live?"
>
> (Lina Sandell, *The Song Goes On*, #149)

3

THE AFFIRMATION

When the Covenant Church affirms that it is evangelical, it proclaims that the new birth in Jesus Christ is essential. We teach that "by the death and resurrection of Jesus Christ, God conquered sin, death, and the devil, offering forgiveness for sin and assuring eternal life for those who follow Christ."[1] New birth is more than the experience of forgiveness and acceptance. It is regeneration and the gift of eternal life. This life has the qualities of love and righteousness as well as joy and peace.

Jesus said to Nicodemus, "No one can see the kingdom of God without being born from above" (John 3:3). To enter the kingdom is not only to have a right relationship with God but to be enlisted in Christ's service. God's purposes entail the transformation of persons, as well as the transformation of God's world into a place of truth, justice, and peace.

As an evangelical church we believe that conversion results in eternal life. Conversion can be defined as the act by which a person turns with repentance and faith from sin to God. Conversion involves a conscious rejection of the life of sin and involves a com-

The Necessity of New Birth

mitment of faith. Eternal life is not given through assent to creeds alone, but through a personal commitment to Jesus Christ.

Such a high doctrine of conversion does not mean that all believers have dramatic conversion experiences. While no one remembers the moment of physical birth, one's present life is evidence of its occurrence. So a person may be truly converted even though he or she has no memory of the moment of new birth. The vitality of life is the proof of birth, not its memory or recollection.

It is the will of God that all should be redeemed: "The Lord is not slow about his promise, as some think of slowness, but is patient with you, not wanting any to perish, but all to come to repentance" (2 Peter 3:9). Yet it is only through the grace of Christ that we can be saved. Our Savior declared, "I am the way, and the truth, and the life. No one comes to the Father except through me" (John 14:6). The apostles concurred: "There is salvation in no one else, for there is no other name under heaven given among mortals by which we must be saved" (Acts 4:12). The Covenant Church shares God's concern for the salvation of all, but accepts God's word that only those converted to Jesus Christ shall be saved.

The new birth, however, is only the beginning of life. Growing to maturity in Christ is a lifelong process called sanctification. Being formed in Christ is the goal, for both individuals and communities of believers. The Apostle Paul agonized as a woman in labor, that believers might express Christ's character and goodness in their whole being (Galatians 4:19).

On this journey of being transformed by the Holy Spirit into Christ's likeness, God's people experience and express love for God and others. Healthy and effective spiritual growth takes place in the context of relationships, both within and beyond peer groups. The desired outcome of this formational process is described by the Apostle Paul: "until all of us come to the unity of the faith and of the knowledge of the Son of God, to maturity, to the measure of the full stature of Christ" (Ephesians 4:13).

Being a disciple of Jesus implies costly obedience to all of his teachings. Such obedience, together with the Spirit's work in us, equips us to do the work of the kingdom, giving witness to the good news and serving others in Jesus's name.

Though there is no state of final perfection in this life, there is a process of growth from beginning to end. This growth is as much a gift of God as the gift of life itself (Galatians 3:3). Together with the gifts of life and growth, the child of God receives the gifts of assurance of salvation and confidence in the faith. The Apostle Paul declares: "I am confident of this, that the one who began a good work among you will bring it to completion by the day of Jesus Christ" (Philippians 1:6).

As there is no new birth without repentance and faith, so there is no healthy spiritual growth without a life of discipline. Discipline is the cultivation and nurture of the spiritual life in both its personal and corporate dimensions. Public worship, participation in the sacraments, prayer, Bible study, service to others, stewardship, fellowship, and other spiritual disciplines all enhance the Christian's growth. A life of discipline prepares us individually and communally for passionate engagement in the work of Christ in our world. It is through transformed people that God transforms our world. It is for this reason we are called into new life. A life of discipline seeks to avoid moral and spiritual indifference on the one hand and oppressive legalism on the other.

In his letter to the Ephesians, the Apostle Paul declares: "You were taught to put away your former way of life, your old self, corrupt and deluded by its lusts, and to be renewed in the spirit of your minds, and to clothe yourselves with the new self, created according to the likeness of God in true righteousness and holiness" (Ephesians 4:22-24).

While the pursuit of holy living does not earn God's favor, it pleases God. It allows the Spirit to fill the Christian with joy and makes the Christian an effective agent of reconciliation.

3

THEOLOGICAL REFLECTION

Were you to visit a nineteenth-century Covenant church, you would likely be greeted with the words, "Are you living now in Jesus?" This favored question of our Covenant mothers and fathers is an evangelical one. It both assumes the salvific power of new birth in Jesus Christ and inquires into the ongoing transformative power of Christ in the life of believers. New birth is "necessary" precisely because we believe it is salvific and the pathway to becoming co-workers with Christ. New birth is a gift from God that, as our second affirmation claims, enlists us in Christ's service to work toward the redemption of all. Those who are "living now in Jesus" work on behalf of this good news.

This chapter echoes the celebratory and evangelistic spirit of new birth in Christ by reflecting on the gift of eternal life as it encompasses the spectrum of God's renewing work in us. Renewal includes new birth, and it also includes new life. New birth refers to conversion as "that act by which a person turns with repentance and faith from sin to God," as stated in the second affirmation. It is a personal commitment to Jesus Christ and a conscious rejection of sin. New life is about the lifelong process of growing to maturity in Christ, or sanctification. New life is about being equipped for being Christ's disciples. New birth and new life are, of course, related as God's offer of grace and work of sanctification. The church affirms this relationship through the sacrament of baptism. Baptism communally ritualizes the second affirmation in its commitments to new birth and new life, to God's gift and our response, and to conversion and discipleship. Along with new birth as conversion and new life as forming disciples, this chapter engages baptism as it unites one's personal commitment to Jesus Christ and the whole mission of the church to do the "passionate...work of Christ in our world," as the second affirmation states.

NEW BIRTH: CONVERSION

In John 3, Nicodemus comes to Jesus and asks what one must do to be born a second time. Jesus answers in the words so familiar to us, "Very truly, I tell you, no one can enter the kingdom of God without being born of water and Spirit.... You must be born from above" (vv. 5, 7). In this passage, Jesus tells Nicodemus that all who believe in Jesus Christ are born anew. They receive eternal life because they believe that God sent his Son to save the world from sin.

Christians believe that this new birth to which Jesus refers is a kind of conversion, but what does conversion entail? How does the New Testament talk about conversion? And, why is it "necessary"? The New Testament writers are not wary of making large claims for what has been accomplished through the death and resurrection of Jesus. Motivated by God's unlimited love for the world (John 3:16), Christ's death for our sins is instrumental in breaking

The Necessity of New Birth

the power of the "present evil age" (Galatians 1:4). The ultimate consequence is that creation itself will be liberated from decay and enjoy the "freedom of the glory of the children of God" (Romans 8:21). There will be a new heaven and a new earth where God, having made all things new, will dwell with men and women (Revelation 21:1-5). Through Christ, God is reclaiming God's creation, bringing it out of the shadows of sin and death into fullness of life. It is in this context that we proclaim the necessity of the new birth for each and every individual. If human beings are to participate in God's reclamation of the marred and damaged creation of which they are a part, they too must be made new. If human beings are to enter into life that is eternal, they too must be liberated from death. If human beings are to become dwelling places for God (John 14:23, Romans 8:9), they must be forgiven their sins and set free. It is only from such radical new beginnings that the common life as God's people flows, marked by the presence and the power of the Holy Spirit, which demonstrates the wider hope for the whole world (Romans 8:20, James 1:18).

It is therefore unsurprising that the New Testament contains a cluster of metaphors used to describe conversion that convey its equivalence to the act of creation itself. Conversion is of such significance that the original divine gift of life provides a fitting analogue for the divine gift of new life. Paul speaks plainly of the person in Christ as a new creation (2 Corinthians 5:17, Galatians 6:15). He also compares God's act of converting Gentiles through his own ministry to the calling into being of things that do not exist (Romans 4:17, 1 Corinthians 1:26). The image of new birth itself emphasizes the same truth. When Jesus says, "You must be born from above" (John 3:3, 7), he thereby points out that there is nothing within current human existence that can serve as a basis for new life in him. It requires the gift from God of a new origin and source of life: "What is born of flesh is flesh, and what is born of the Spirit is spirit" (John 3:6). Those ransomed by the blood of Jesus from futile ways, inherited according to usual human patterns of descent (1 Peter 1:18-19), now enjoy the living hope granted in Christ by new birth (1 Peter 1:3). To be converted is to be re-shaped by God the Holy Spirit to such a degree that to speak of changing or transforming the existing person is wholly inadequate. There comes into being not merely a changed person but a new person. The corollary of this creation of a new person is the death of the old one. To walk in newness of life can result only from sharing in Christ's death (Romans 6:3, 6). Paul can say that, since he has been crucified with Christ, he no longer lives but rather Christ lives in him (Galatians 2:19-20). If there is a danger here of speaking in a way that might suggest the mere obliteration of the individual, this is a risk that Paul seems fully prepared to take. For far from denoting any divine lack of regard for the individual, the radical discontinuity of conversion springs from the work of the Son of God "who loved me and gave himself for me" (Galatians 2:20). Secure in this love, Paul and the other New Testament writers can locate the essential personhood of the individual in the creator God who first gave life and then new life. Paradoxically, it is only in leaving behind the self in conversion that the self can be found: "Those who want to save their life will lose it, and those who lose their life for my sake will find it" (Matthew 16:25).

To enter into this radical new birth is a matter of faith in Jesus

Christ: "This is the work of God, that you believe in him whom he has sent" (John 6:29). Such faith finds its focus in the death and resurrection of Jesus, where sin and death are defeated, and such faith unites us with Christ and grants us his righteousness. In a world where "there is no one who is righteous, not even one" (Romans 3:10), righteousness is graciously given as a gift by God to those who trust in the sacrificial death of Jesus (Romans 3:21-26). After the pattern of Abraham, who "believed God and it was reckoned to him as righteousness" (Romans 4:3, Genesis 15:6), the believer is declared righteous and granted peace with God (Romans 5:1). The image is that of a verdict in a court of law, but this does not mean that the righteousness given to the believer is a mere legal fiction. It is not the case that the believer is declared righteous when in fact still guilty, a shabby reality shielded by a splendid cloak of righteousness passed on from Christ. For the righteousness of Christ is not an object or a substance transferred from him to the believer. It is rather *part of who he is*. He is "for us wisdom from God, and righteousness and sanctification and redemption" (1 Corinthians 1:30). It is in him that we become the righteousness of God (2 Corinthians 5:21). Paul's language of righteousness by faith must therefore be heard in conjunction with his emphasis on the union of the believer with Christ. Faith unites us with Christ, making his presence a reality, and since he is righteous, then in him we too are righteous. In this way we are brought back again to the necessity of new birth. When Christ begins to live in a person, there is a new creation, born from above, whence comes the fitting question, "Are you living now in Jesus?"

Living in Jesus, or receiving new birth, is also to become part of God's people. The necessity of new life for the individual, which cannot be based on the person who already exists, is matched at the communal level by divine disregard for all human structures, boundaries, and distinctions. The gift of faith in Jesus is not channeled according to ethnicity, social status, or gender (Galatians 3:28, Revelation 7:9), but rests upon God's freely given grace that creates one people (1 Corinthians 12:12-13). To be converted is to enter into a society that recognizes no form of human worthiness or identity as its basis, only the love of God in Christ for each person. New birth is new identity. To be converted is to allow this value to structure our attitudes and patterns of behavior. To be converted is to commit oneself to the life and work of the church as it seeks to participate in the expression of this untrammeled divine love for the world. In doing so, the church does nothing less than continue the priorities of Jesus made plain in his earthly ministry. The poor, the captive, the blind, and the oppressed are the focus of his purpose, those who are favored by God but not by humans (Luke 4:18-19). This focus is reflected in his meals with tax collectors and sinners, in his healing of the sick, in his freeing of those possessed by demonic forces. It is manifest in his willingness to endure hostility and controversy that God's compassion might be known by all. Above all, it is displayed in his self-giving love: "For the Son of Man came not to be served but to serve, and to give his life a ransom for many" (Mark 10:45). In all of this we are provided the clearest picture of the life of those who have received new birth. If new birth unites us with Christ, making us one with him and with fellow believers, then its consequence will be that we grow to become like him: "Every good tree bears good fruit" (Matthew 7:17-19).

Such fruitful growth takes place as we exercise our ministry as believers. If we find the clearest picture of a life free from the power of sin in the ministry of Jesus, then it is unsurprising that new birth is manifested in active discipleship. The call of Jesus to the Galilean fishermen was a practical one: Follow me to a life of witness to the good news and of serving others (Mark 1:16-20). It is no coincidence that Paul describes his ministry as a call to be an apostle (Romans 1:1, 1 Corinthians 1:1, Galatians 1:15), but also uses the language of calling more frequently than any other vocabulary to describe the conversion of believers (Romans 1:7, 1 Corinthians 1:24). Although there are particular ministries in the church for which specific individuals are chosen, ministry is to be shared by all. Those who have been granted new birth must be able to stand with Peter, who, despite considerable frailties, was able honestly to say, "Look, we have left everything and followed you" (Mark 10:28). This is not to demand that all undergo identical experiences. It is rather to recognize the sovereign work of the Spirit, which is like the wind. It blows where it chooses, yet it is heard and its effects are seen (John 3:8).

While the analogy by Jesus between the wind and the Spirit draws our attention to the limits of what can be *said* about new birth and conversion, we can also celebrate the many ways that persons come to Christ and respond to the good news that God loved us so much that God sent his Son for us. This universal truth takes particularity in the variety of ways that persons come to know God. One only need to walk through the book of Acts to see that the nature of new birth takes such varied forms as the conversions of the Ethiopian eunuch (Acts 8:27-39), Saul of Tarsus (Acts 9:1-19), Cornelius (Acts 10), Lydia (Acts 16:14-15), and the Philippian jailer (Acts 16:25-34). The important aspect in all of these stories is that conversion is vital to new life in Christ because those who respond to God in faith are drawn into the gospel and transformed by its power. They are given new life and charged with Jesus's words: "Go therefore and make disciples of all nations, baptizing them in the name of the Father and of the Son and of the Holy Spirit" (Matthew 28:19).

NEW LIFE: GO THEREFORE AND MAKE DISCIPLES

Just as new birth is essential for salvation, this new birth necessitates a new way of living that we call Christian discipleship. Discipleship is both about growing in Christ (sanctification) and about proclaiming the good news of Christ (evangelism). We grow by submitting ourselves to God and one another, and to this end, the church's engagement in Christian formation is critical. Christian formation equips us to do Christ's work of evangelism and to be effective agents of forgiveness and reconciliation.

Although new birth can be declared and affirmed in a simple testimony, new birth initiates a dynamic journey of Christian discipleship. This dynamic journey is seen in the momentary behaviors of individuals, in the long-term processes of whole communities, and in the great narrative of the whole Christian church. As a dynamic journey, new life in Christ is more than simply naming yourself a Christian or attending church or gatherings. The journey as a whole becomes a unique commentary on the goodness and glory of God in our lives.

Our new life in Christ is characterized by the ongoing work

of salvation in the life of the believer (Philippians 2). The power of the gospel opens new opportunities at all levels of personhood: our self-awareness (identity), our behavioral contributions to community (significance), and our sense of direction and hope (purpose). At each of these levels, the gospel declares: we are treasured as God's children; we have gifts and are significant participants in the work of the kingdom; and we have a hope that sets our lives on a trajectory that even now points to God's greater glory.

At each stage of life—from infancy to adolescence, adulthood, and into the later years—God in Christ provides ways for us to live out the gospel and to declare that we are no longer slaves to sinful tendencies but can live in the glory of new life in Christ. Young or old, regardless of when we enter new life, we are given opportunities to live out our new identity, significance, and purpose for God's glory. Christian formation for all ages becomes a critical vocation of the church. From children's Sunday school to confirmation to adult formation and ongoing learning, Christian formation requires rigor and intentionality to form people to do the passionate work of Christ in the world. The way we see the world and do the church's mission will change through rigorous formation. Prayer will be flavored by a real sense of God's presence and concern for others and for ourselves. Service will heighten our sense of God's work in the greater world, reveal God's work in others, and provide us with a sense of being God's hands and feet in the world. Scripture reading will provide a similar sense of God's presence with us, a sense for others from whom and for whom the word speaks, a profound sense of ourselves as participants in the story of the word. Church attendance will have a new meaning where we gather before God in worship with fellow believers in time-honored corporate worship, personal formation, and service. All of these take shape in different ways according to varying levels of Christian maturity, yet all are ways that we grow in our new life in Christ. New life means attending to these varying aspects of formation—in ourselves and in one another.

Experiencing new birth does not mean we will automatically live in Christ-likeness. Our natural tendency is to live in sin. A struggle exists between the old and the new (Romans 7). Just as new life is afforded at every developmental stage (age) and at every level of personhood (identity, significance, and purpose), so the struggle exists between the old and the new within us. Herein is the journey of working out our salvation in fear and trembling (Philippians 2:12). Each day provides opportunities to live out the new life or remain in the old. At times we fall, and at other times God is glorified in our lives. But it doesn't end with "sometimes we sin and sometimes we don't." If this were true, our life would be filled with constant contradictions between affirming sin and affirming Christ (Romans 7:24-25). We need not stay in our sin. In the place of sin, Christ provides us a way to repent (turn around) and testify to the death of sin and the resurrection of Christ in our life (Romans 5, 6, 8). We can be "overcomers" (Romans 12:21; 1 John 5:1-5), allowing Christ to transform us (Romans 12:1-2) and developing patterns of being and doing that show that we are living now in Jesus. When we do sin, we must remember that God's glory and goodness are revealed in the acts of repentance and confession and in the acts of forgiveness and reconciliation. These constitute the heart of the new life that follows new birth and operates in how we enact this with one another. With humble thankfulness we press on to live the new life in Christ. This takes time, practice, and discipline so that our overall journey becomes the greater commentary on the power of Christ to transform lives.

NEW COMMUNITY: BAPTIZING THEM IN THE NAME OF THE FATHER AND OF THE SON AND OF THE HOLY SPIRIT

One of the unique characteristics of the Covenant is that we hold a high view of conversion, and we cherish the sacrament of baptism in both infant and believer modes. Committed to the full testimony of Scripture, the Covenant retains the necessity of personal acceptance of faith. When we baptize believers, we rejoice with the person who commits their life to Christ. Baptism affirms the gift of grace shown, as John 3:16 says, in God's gift of his Son. When we baptize infants, we marvel at God's grace present and extended to us before we can act in faith.

Baptism is the way that the church celebrates the whole spectrum of God's renewing activity in the life of individuals and the church. Whether the mode be infant or believer, baptism is a community's response to the gift of new birth and the promise to form persons to live new lives as disciples of Jesus Christ. The vows made by the congregation affirm the importance of sanctification in growing mature Christians or, in the case of infants, a devotion to forming the child in the midst of Christian community. *Together* the practice of both modes is meant to reflect the moments of God's saving work—both backward and forward—as the offer of newness for all creation. Baptismal confessions look back to God's work in creation, Israel, the incarnation, Christ's death and resurrection as well as anticipate God's ongoing activity toward the end when all things will be made new.

In the economy of salvation revealed in Scripture, baptism is presented as God's work embodied in creation. The spiritual and physical (Spirit and water) are encompassing facets of the same divine work. When Jesus introduces "birth from above" to Nicodemus, he speaks cryptically: "No one can enter the kingdom of God without being born of water and Spirit" (John 3:5). Yet there is clarity and promise as well. The "kingdom of God" is a new age of God's rule inaugurated by Jesus the Messiah within the created realm. Entrance into this realm, Jesus says, requires a fresh start, namely birth by water and by Spirit. Christians throughout time have taken this to mean a holistic response to the gospel.

A look at Jesus's own baptism offers further clarity on the reality of water and Spirit woven together for God's purposes of redemption. Matthew's account begins by describing John the Baptist's prophetic call to God's people to repent, and the subsequent response of the Judean masses who came to be "baptized by him in the river Jordan, confessing their sins" (Matthew 3:6). John's washing of repentance was an invitation for the people of Israel to return to their roots, to the wilderness place where God acted in mighty ways to accomplish their salvation through water and the covenant. In the wilderness, the people of Israel stood empty-handed and wholly dependent upon their God to do for them what they could not do for themselves. Here in the desert, in the waters of renewal, God would redefine them as God's covenant people; and here also is the place where Jesus begins his own mission: "Jesus came from Galilee to John at the Jordan, to be baptized by him"

The Necessity of New Birth

(Matthew 3:13).

Jesus's choice of baptism by John is a shocking political move for one who has already been defined as the promised Messiah, the virgin-born *Emmanuel*. One doesn't typically launch a political campaign for high office and then publicly sign up for an entry-level community college class on political science! Yet here is Jesus, in apparent disregard for his credentials, wading into the muddy waters with the unwashed masses. John attempts to dissuade him. "I need to be baptized by you, and do you come to me?" he asks. Jesus responds, "Let it be so now; for it is proper for us in this way to fulfill all righteousness" (Matthew 3:14-15). This "let it be so" rightly echoes the "let there be" of the Creator in Genesis 1. Jesus's baptism signals a new beginning for the world and for humanity. Jesus intends to be Emmanuel (God-with-us) to the uttermost. He descends to the level of solidarity with fallen humanity, sinking down into the waters of repentance, so that God's plan of setting things right can be fulfilled within the human story. Christ's baptism is not mere play-acting; it is not an empty ritual of some alternate spiritual reality. It is the very embodiment of God's redemptive plan for the world.

Paul later indicates that the deep identification of Jesus with us in baptism becomes reciprocal in our baptism: "Therefore we have been buried with him by baptism into death, so that, just as Christ was raised from the dead by the glory of the Father, we too might walk in newness of life" (Romans 6:4). Baptism marks a fresh start, yes, for the mission of Jesus, but also for all those who come to share in his mission through baptism. Christ participates in our life, he declares solidarity with our rebellious and broken cause,

The Necessity of New Birth

and we, by entering the same sanctified waters, come to participate in his death and resurrection to new life. Of course, this birth does not come by water alone, but by "water and Spirit" (John 3:5). Regeneration is a matter of the work of the Creator Spirit who once hovered maternally "over the face of the waters" (Genesis 1:2) at the dawn of creation. When Jesus steps out of the Jordan, "the heavens were opened to him, and he saw the Spirit of God descending like a dove and alighting on him" (Matthew 3:16). This baptismal moment signals the definitive act of divine judgment and salvation, now centered in the life of a single person. Jesus responds by taking up his cross, beginning the *missio Dei* (sending of God) for the Son of God.

Baptism marks the beginning of something new—a new humanity and a new world. In baptism, we are incorporated into the life of the one who is in full fellowship with the Father through the Spirit, so much so that his fellowship becomes ours: "God has sent the Spirit of his Son into our hearts, crying, 'Abba, Father'" (Galatians 4:6). Inasmuch as Christ's family identity becomes ours in baptism, so does Christ's mission. Since baptism is Christ's "ordination" to ministry, it is also ours. All who are baptized into Jesus (as he was baptized into our humanity) become participants in his life, death, and resurrection mission for the world (Romans 6:3-7).

Baptism opens the door to full priestly ministry for the people of God. It encompasses both new birth and new life for individuals and for the people of God. Infant baptism celebrates the sole initiative of God in extending the gift of faith. Believer baptism celebrates repentance and conversion. Both celebrate the commitment to new life. *The Covenant Book of Worship* refers to the unity of

The Necessity of New Birth

baptism and teaching in the process of maturing in faith, of becoming disciples (Matthew 28:18-20). We baptize in God's name, and in doing so claim the good news that God calls even formidable, calloused fiddle players like Carl August Björk into his tender care.

NOTES

1. From *The Journey: A Leader's Guide for Discipleship/Confirmation* (Chicago: Covenant Publications, 2001).

FOR FURTHER READING

Frisk, Donald C. *The New Life in Christ.* Chicago: Covenant Publications, 1969.

Hooker, Morna D. "Interchange and Suffering." In *Suffering and Martyrdom in the New Testament.* Edited by William Horbury and Brian McNeil, 70-83. Cambridge: Cambridge University Press, 1981.

Lewis, C. S. *Mere Christianity.* San Francisco: HarperOne, 2001.

Petersen, Johanna Eleonora. "The Nature and Necessity of the New Creature in Christ." In *The Life of Lady Johanna Eleonora Petersen, Written by Herself.* Edited by Barbara Becker-Cantarino. Translated by Francis Oakley. Chicago: The University of Chicago Press, 2005.

Snodgrass, Klyne, ed. *Ex Auditu: An International Journal for the Theological Interpretation of Scripture* 25, Conversion (2009).

_____. *Ex Auditu: An International Journal for the Theological Interpretation of Scripture* 26, Atonement (2010).

Weld, Wayne, ed. *The Covenant Quarterly* (Covenant Publications) 53-54, A Study on Baptism (November 1995–February 1996).

4

A Commitment to the Whole Mission of the Church

HISTORICAL ROOTS

From its inception, people in the Covenant Church have been friends of mission. Experiencing new spiritual birth during the sweeping movements of European renewal during the nineteenth century, a group of believers dedicated themselves to the mission of pursuing together the new life in Christ. The name they chose for themselves was "Mission Friends." It was out of this holy passion that Mission Friends who immigrated to the United States later formed the Evangelical Covenant Church. The sense of mission of this group was deeply rooted in Pietism's path-breaking activism in Protestant evangelism and social ministries at home and around the globe. This spirit was captured in August Hermann Francke's assertion that Christians should live intentionally for "God's glory and neighbor's good." Words chiseled into a stone in the foundation of Old Main at North Park University in Chicago by the graduating class of 1911 captures the affirmation succinctly:

"For God and Humanity." Mission as personal devotion to Christ and compassion for others has been at the core of the denomination's identity ever since.

Stories of this commitment to mission of the new life in Christ among the Mission Friends abound. One story with a long legacy, occurring at the beginning of the spiritual stirrings that led to the Covenant Church, illustrates the commitment to the whole mission of the church. Maria Nilsdotter was a peasant woman in rural Sweden, unhappily married to an alcoholic ironworker who abused her. She sought help from the parish pastor, a Pietist. In addition to his care, the pastor encouraged her to read the Bible and devotional literature together with other women in the district. This led to her conversion in 1846. To prevent her from attending the small group conventicles, Maria's husband on occasion would tie her to the iron post of her kitchen stove. He died not long after, and Maria began to think about what she could contribute to mission.

At this time there were many orphaned children who were sold to the lowest bidder, ostensibly to be raised and cared for by foster families. In reality, it was often a form of abusive child labor with horrid conditions and frequent beatings. Along with another widow, Birgitta Olsson, Maria was determined to rescue these children from indentured servitude by purchasing as many as she could. So she and Birgitta began to sew and knit, selling their handiwork for needed funds. As her household grew with young boys and girls added to her own brood of children, Maria raised the money to build an orphanage and then a small school adjacent to her small dwelling. The area was known as *Vall* (meadow), her farm was called *Nyvall* (new meadow), and she became known and

A Commitment to the Whole Mission of the Church

revered as *Mor i Vall* (Mother in Vall). The buildings still stand in Värmland, much as they were when Maria labored so faithfully.

Maria's legacy lies not only in the lives of these forgotten children and their descendants. She was instrumental in her son's dramatic conversion in 1849 following a life-threatening logging accident. Carl Johan Nyvall became the leading Mission Friend preacher in northwestern Sweden, was one of the founders of the Covenant Church in Sweden in 1878, and made four extended visits to the United States before his death in 1904. His presence was very important at the organization of the Covenant in Chicago in 1885. Maria's grandson was David Nyvall, first president of North Park College and the church's most formative intellectual leader. The son of Maria's co-worker, Birgitta, was Olof Olsson, who became president of Augustana College in Rock Island, Illinois. An early pastor and leader of the Augustana Synod of the Lutheran Church, he was a warm friend to many Covenanters. The impact of one person's obedience to God's mission continues through many generations of Covenanters.

Following the famous Columbian Exposition held in Chicago in 1893, the World's Parliament of Religions brought together an impressive group of leaders from the sixteen major religions of the time. Although the Swedish Evangelical Mission Covenant was not yet ten years old, David Nyvall and others sought to represent the young movement to the global ecumenical audience. An excerpt of his report reads, "The Covenant is not a church organization in the ordinary sense, but a mission society having churches as its members. These churches have consolidated because of the missionary spirit which led them to missionary enterprises too large for any single church to undertake." At a time when Protestantism divisiveness was strident, Nyvall's attendance and address at the World's Parliament of Religions was a challenging and bold move in the eyes of many Christians (including some Covenanters!). Yet for him and many others, the missional identity of the Covenant meant a devotion to Christ that went beyond creedal differences. Being a Mission Friend meant extending the impact of Christ's compassion beyond ethnic and theological boundaries. A commitment to evangelism and compassion for all continues to work in the denominational heart.

The clear impetus for the personal and corporate mission of Covenant Mission Friends emerged from their high regard for Scripture. Together the great commission (Matthew 28:19-20) and the great commandment (Matthew 22:37-40) were included when Covenanters considered their response to the divine question, "Whom shall I send, and who will go for us?" Like Isaiah, Covenanters continue to answer, "Here am I; send me!" (Isaiah 6:8). Another important story in Covenant mission history is that of Peter Matson. In 1888 as a young Swedish immigrant out in the fields of his family's Minnesota farm, Matson experienced an unmistakable sense that God was calling him into missionary service. There by a haystack he knelt in prayer for some time, promising that he would honor God in obedience if he could go abroad, or if not, promising to give 50 percent of his income to missions. This led Matson to E. A. Skogsbergh's school in Minneapolis (which became the Covenant school, now North Park, in 1891) and seminary education in Chicago. In 1890 at the age of twenty-three Matson became one of the first Covenant missionaries sent to China. Follow-

A Commitment to the Whole Mission of the Church

ing the directives of Hudson Taylor's mission, to whom Covenant missionaries were first seconded, Matson exchanged his western garb for Chinese clothing and proceeded to the interior province of Hupeh where he endured physical hardships and hostilities. In spite of serious challenges, he became fluent in Chinese and expanded Covenant ministries to embrace evangelism, education, and health care. Matson's vision was for the church's whole mission to people as individuals, confronting the systemic difficulties in their lives. His impact at home has shaped the denomination's orientation to mission both globally and locally.

In Matson's later years he served as an adviser to the head of world mission of the Swedish Covenant Church when that group was beginning its work in Congo. At the 1934 Annual Meeting of the North American Covenant, in the midst of a global economic depression, the motion came to consider opening a new field in Congo in conjunction with the work of the Swedish Covenant. At age sixty-six Matson immediately jumped out of his front-row seat onto the platform, "pouring out all the passion of his burning soul in favor of the new missionary enterprise which he fully believed was a commission of the Lord God." The later reports of the work of God in Congo brought him to tears. Through God's grace the legacy of the Covenant's work in China, in Congo, and in many other countries continues today with churches and members far outnumbering the original sending mission.

The commitment to the whole mission of church embraces evangelism and discipleship, caring for the physical, spiritual, and emotional needs of all. Our commitment advocates for the full participation of women in ministry and leadership. Our commitment

A Commitment to the Whole Mission of the Church

addresses the suffering of the human and non-human creation for which we are responsible. We continually respond to the great commandment, asking, "Who is my neighbor?" We remain rooted in the great commission, asking, "Where shall I go?" The Covenant's vision and vigilance is constant, rooted in the words of Jesus to seek the lost and love the neighbor in his name. Covenant pastor and hymn writer, Bryan Jeffery Leech, has captured this divine mandate:

> Through all the world let everyone embrace
> the gift of grace!
> May Christ's great light consume
> our cities' darkest gloom,
> May Christ's love efface hostilities of race.
> Through all the world let everyone embrace
> the gift of grace!
>
> If all the world in every part shall hear
> and God revere,
> We must be moved to care
> and in his name to share
> The liberating word which must be told abroad.
> Then all the world in every part shall hear
> and God revere!
>
> (*The Covenant Hymnal: A Worshipbook*, #699)

4

THE AFFIRMATION

The Covenant Church has always been characterized by its involvement in mission. The earliest name attributed to Covenanters was "Mission Friends," people who covenanted together for the purpose of common mission both far and near. They understood the work of mission to be evangelism and Christian formation, as well as the benevolent ministries of compassion and justice in the face of suffering and oppression. This is the legacy of Pietism, which was instrumental in pioneering the Protestant missionary movement. An early Pietist, August Hermann Francke (1663-1727) described this when he said that the Christian lives for God's glory and the good of one's neighbor. At Halle in Germany, Francke was instrumental in developing a Pietist university that educated pastors, teachers, and missionaries. Pietists there founded orphanages, a hospital, a pharmacy, a printing press, and a great library devoted to a global vision of Christian service. We remain a community of friends committed to this whole mission of the church.

Jesus made it clear that if his followers were to love him, they must keep his commandments. He said, "'You shall love the Lord your God with all your heart, and with all your soul, and with all your mind.' This is the greatest and first commandment. And a second is like it: 'You shall love your neighbor as yourself.' On these two commandments hang all the law and the prophets" (Matthew 22:37-40). This is the great commandment.

The Covenant Church is also committed to the great commission of Jesus Christ: "Go therefore and make disciples of all nations, baptizing them in the name of the Father and of the Son and of the Holy Spirit, and teaching them to obey everything that I have commanded you" (Matthew 28:19-20).

Established by the gospel and grace of Jesus Christ, the church exists by doing mission—the great commission and the great commandment—as fire exists by burning. The church's mission is faith active in love, and the two cannot be separated without diminishing the gospel. As Christ's representative in the world, the church is to be an agent of grace, entrusted with the message of reconciliation, hope, justice, and peace. At the end of his life, Jesus declared his disciples his friends, meaning they shared with him a common passion for his mission in the world (John 15:13-15). Covenanters, as Mission Friends, have broadly understood mission to be the befriending of others, and all that God has created, in the name of the One who first befriended us.

Covenanters, like all Christians, are called to proclaim this good news with their lives and words, and by the love and integrity of their communities. In faithful witness, the lost are found in Christ. In acts of generosity and compassion, people are ministered to and justice is proclaimed. In the work of evangelism and mission, we seek to embody the presence of Jesus Christ with head, hands, voice, and heart. Jesus called on his disciples to carry their own crosses, and in this joyful way of suffering and service we embody his ministry of reconciliation and proclaim the reality of the kingdom, which extends to every person in every land and to the whole of creation. The Covenant Church, therefore, is "committed to reaching across boundaries of race, ethnicity, culture, gender, age, and status in the cultivation of communities of life and service."[1] This mission belongs to the whole church, the spiritual priesthood of all believers—women and men, young and old, laity and clergy.

The Covenant Church seeks to hold together proclamation and compassion, personal witness and social justice, service and stewardship in all areas of life. God makes all things new and calls God's followers to share this mission. Those who neither know nor love the Lord Jesus as well as those enduring poverty, suffering, inequality, and injustice cannot be ignored. In the incarnation of Jesus Christ, "God was pleased to reconcile to himself all things, whether on earth or in heaven, by making peace through the blood of his cross" (Colossians 1:20). This bears witness to God's boundless passion for both the souls and earthly lives of all people, and for all that God has made. When we address not only the consequences but also the causes of suffering, we live out what it means to be the body of Christ in the world.

4

THEOLOGICAL REFLECTION

In the streets of India, young girls are sold every day to persons who enslave them indefinitely. In the Democratic Republic of the Congo, civil wars threaten the lives of its citizens and the stability of its government. In the United States, nearly one in four children are at risk of hunger. These injustices are not new, nor are they confined to the geographic regions named. The abusers, victims, oppressors, and captives are always with us, and it is in the midst of these people that we are co-workers with Christ, pleading with God, "thy kingdom come."

Mission is the work of the whole church on behalf of the kingdom of God. It is working with Christ for peace, reconciliation, justice, and evangelism. Mission encompasses freeing the captives, healing the sick, feeding the hungry, and telling the good news. It is life-long work, and it is holistic.

The holistic dimension of mission is reflected in the vision statements of Covenant ministries. "Our charge is to love, serve, and work together with the poor, the powerless, and the marginalized," reads the statement of Covenant World Relief. Congoleseinspired Paul Carlson Partnership "works together with people in places of deep poverty to catalyze the development of sustainable communities through economic development. In the process, we invest in the social systems that are necessary for healthy families and workers, primarily health care and education. We also address infrastructure problems that impede development, including transportation systems, power, and water." The Department of Compassion, Mercy, and Justice stretches "far and wide as the Evangelical Covenant Church responds to domestic and global needs. This department [builds] on that strong foundation and continues to lead and coordinate efforts in the area of justice in order to be the heart, hands, and feet of Christ." The vision of the Department of World Mission reflects the vision statement of the Evangelical Covenant Church: "to see more disciples among more populations in a more caring and just world."

These salient statements point to an incontrovertible reality: the Covenant Church lives out its faith by doing mission. It is central to our history and identity as disciples of Jesus Christ. We say it in many ways: For God's glory, and neighbor's good. All that matters is faith acting in love (Galatians 5:6). A ministry of head, heart, and hands. We are missional Pietists.

When we affirm the great commandment we engage in the whole mission of the church. But what exactly do we mean when we say we are a people committed to the whole mission of the church? What are the theological and practical ways we understand mission? This chapter reflects on the third affirmation by examining our theology of advancing God's kingdom, the centrality of relationships and reconciliation, and our belief in holistic evangelism.

A Commitment to the Whole Mission of the Church

ADVANCING GOD'S KINGDOM

Mission belongs to God. As people of the word, Covenanters understand that God is the loving initiator of mission and is already at work in the world. God demonstrates this initiation of mission in attitude, action, and character throughout the written revelation of both the Old and New Testaments. The earliest image of God's hovering Spirit portrays a compassionate attitude of concern that out of chaos would come created order. This impulse to initiate a mission of compassion in the chaos of brokenness is reflected in God's pursuant question to the man and woman in hiding: "Where are you?" (Genesis 3:9). God's attitude of mercy prompts the call to restoration and relationship, and it extends today to all shamed, guilty, self-righteous, and otherwise separated people. Scripture records numerous examples of God's initiation of love and compassion, directed toward humanity in the face of rejection, indifference, and occasional obedience.

God calls people as partners in mission who demonstrate God's attitude toward creation. Mission partners stand in constant need of reminders that their participation must come from the attitudes of the heart and not merely following prescribed forms. The question God asked Jonah comes to all who would follow in this mission: "Should I not be concerned?" (Jonah 4:11). The loving heart of this *missio Dei* calls Covenanters to model their involvement after God's attitude of compassion with Christ-like love.

Along with attitude, the Bible also records the actions of God who initiated this mission. God spoke. God created. God walked in the garden. God saw. God heard. God performed miracles. God came as one of us. God also called others into the action of mission as he equipped and sent them. Abram was the first to be called out of all the earth's peoples to both receive a blessing and be a source of blessing to all nations (Genesis 12:1-3). Jesus echoed this theme when he said, "You did not choose me but I chose you. And I appointed you to go and bear fruit" (John 15:16). We are disciples of God's mission, called to bear the fruit of God's initiation of love.

This call to be disciples of God's mission is articulated in the great commandment. Jesus says, "'You shall love the Lord your God with all your heart, and with all your soul, and with all your mind.' This is the greatest and first commandment. And a second is like it: 'You shall love your neighbor as yourself'" (Matthew 22:37-39). Jesus is waiting for his disciples to act and invites the church to join him in his redemptive work for all, and most especially the lost and needy. We are concerned for the powerless, because it is the powerless especially who represent the world for which Christ died (Romans 5:6). From the community of faith in the first century (Acts 2:44-47; 6:1-7; 2 Corinthians 8:3-9) to such inspiring figures as Brother Francis of Assisi, Martin Luther King Jr., and Mother Teresa of Calcutta, whenever there was suffering in the world, the church was there to bear witness to Christ's love for "the least of these" (Matthew 25:40).

Mission is demonstrated in the character of God as the one who sends. God the Father sent the Son. Father and Son sent the Spirit, and together all of the Trinity sends the church into the world (John 20:21-23). The sending of the church expresses the very sending character of God in mission. The global community of God's people, the church, is privileged to be called and sent by God as partners in the work of the whole mission of God to all the

A Commitment to the Whole Mission of the Church

world (Acts 1:8). The Covenant Church therefore is also committed to the great commission of the resurrected Christ: "Go therefore and make disciples of all nations, baptizing them in the name of the Father and of the Son and of the Holy Spirit, and teaching them to obey everything that I have commanded you" (Matthew 28:19-20).

The church's mission is faith active in love, and the two cannot be separated without diminishing the message of the whole gospel. As Christ's representative in the world, the church is to be an agent of grace, entrusted with the message of reconciliation, resurrection, hope, justice, and peace. In its effort to discern how God sends us in our own world, the Covenant has and continues to participate in many ministries, both locally and globally. Our earliest mission field was in Alaska in 1889, and soon after, in 1890, China—a mere five years after the birth of the Covenant. Since then, God has sent persons to partner with groups in the Democratic Republic of the Congo (1937), Mexico (1946), Ecuador (1947), Japan (1949), Taiwan (1952), Colombia (1968), and Thailand (1971). Moreover, beginning in the 1990s, we have entered into ministry with numerous other countries across Africa, Asia, Europe, and Latin America. This impressive list is only impressive in the context of being sent by God and commissioned as co-workers advancing God's kingdom.

Locally, some of our earliest ministries included establishing benevolent institutions. Covenanters have always recognized the need for mission that ministers to the whole person—body, mind, and spirit. In addition to creating the Home of Mercy in Chicago, which later became Swedish Covenant Hospital, over time the mission and ministry of Covenant benevolent institutions has grown to include another hospital (Emanuel Medical Center in Turlock, California), children's homes, retirement communities, and enabling residences for developmentally disabled adults. Further, the Covenant now has churches that have health clinics serving those in impoverished areas. Each of these institutions was created in response to human need and in the context of evangelism for the whole person: care for the sick, shelter for the orphan, support for the elderly, homes for persons who cannot live independently, and resources to sustain health. Sometimes we are sent abroad, sometimes we are sent at home, always we are sent to baptize all in the name of the one who sends—Father, Son, and Holy Spirit—teaching a life of obedience to Christ to all in our path and proclaiming the good news of such a life.

CO-WORKERS WITH CHRIST: RELATIONSHIPS AND RECONCILIATION

Companionship makes for good evangelism. Jesus calls his disciples "friends" because they share with him a common passion for his mission in the world (John 15:13-15). Covenanters, as Mission Friends, have broadly understood mission to be the befriending of others and of all that God has created in the name of the One who first befriended us. This friendship with Christ and with others means that Christians are called to an active faith that moves us toward both the proclamation and the demonstration of God's good news for all.

"Mission Friends" is more than a warm title—it is rooted in Scripture. Luke's Gospel begins with companions. The friendship of Elizabeth and Mary frames one of the greatest gospel hymns of

A Commitment to the Whole Mission of the Church

salvation history:

> My soul magnifies the Lord, and my spirit rejoices in God my Savior, for he has looked with favor on the lowliness of his servant. Surely, from now on all generations will call me blessed; for the Mighty One has done great things for me, and holy is his name. His mercy is for those who fear him from generation to generation. He has shown strength with his arm; he has scattered the proud in the thoughts of their hearts. He has brought down the powerful from their thrones, and lifted up the lowly; he has filled the hungry with good things, and sent the rich away empty. He has helped his servant Israel, in remembrance of his mercy, according to the promise he made to our ancestors, to Abraham and to his descendants forever. (Luke 1:46-55)

These companions, filled with the Holy Spirit, are among the first to proclaim the good news in the form of Christ's mission on earth. Moreover, Luke's Gospel concludes with the story of Cleopas and his companion (24:13-35). As they trudge along the dirt-filled path from Jerusalem to Emmaus, they meet the risen Lord. And when they break bread together, their eyes are opened to Jesus and to the Scriptures. They immediately return to their companions in Jerusalem, proclaiming, "The Lord has risen indeed!"

The making of disciples also thrives in the context of companionship, and the call to be friends with God and others is no easy task. When Jesus speaks of friendship in his last discourse to his disciples, he charges, "Love one another as I have loved you" (John

A Commitment to the Whole Mission of the Church

15:12). Further, "No one has greater love than this, to lay down one's life for one's friends" (John 15:13). The call to lay down one's life for one's friends is sometimes a literal one, and the Covenant remembers its martyrs, seeking to continue their work. November 24, 1964, marks the day that medical missionary Paul Carlson was killed by Simba rebels in the midst of civil war in Congo. When the rebellion began, Carlson evacuated his family to the safety of neighboring Central African Republic. He made the decision to return, however, in order to continue caring for his patients. Captured and held hostage for more than two months, he was killed when a group of rebels opened fire during a rescue by Belgian soldiers of hundreds of hostages. Paul Carlson's sacrifice is a poignant example embodying the call of Jesus to be companions with God's people in its deepest form.

As we seek Christian companionship in mission, we also seek to move beyond superficial connections into deeper relationship with all those who fear God (Psalm 119:63). The challenge of being companions with God's people takes us into diverse places with diverse peoples and requires a commitment to reconciliation, particularly with those who do not have power. From the birth of Christianity in the first century AD and throughout the centuries until today, the church has been engaged in acts of mercy and compassion to the disenfranchised. Because Jesus himself identifies with those who are suffering in this world (Matthew 25:34-40), we who follow Christ are called into conformity with his compassion. Jesus is waiting for his disciples to act and invites the church to join him in his redemptive work for the lost and needy. The church is concerned for the powerless, because it is the powerless who especially

A Commitment to the Whole Mission of the Church

represent the world for whom Christ died (Romans 5:8).

Paul tells the church at Corinth that the same God who "reconciled us to himself through Christ" has also "given us the ministry of reconciliation" (2 Corinthians 5:18). In Christ's death and resurrection God opened the way for sinners to have a renewed relationship with him and, therefore, with one another. Through this personal relationship with Christ, men and women, regardless of ethnicity or culture, can be transformed from their sinful condition into the state designated as the righteousness of God.

Further, Christ's life, death, and resurrection compel Christians to reconsider power as a potential barrier to reconciliation. We find examples of misuse of power in all spheres—economic, social, ethnic, age, and gender—Christ emptying himself and becoming a servant offers the most perfect model for engaging the work of reconciliation. Reconciliation hinges on serving one another, transfering power to the powerless, and breaking down barriers that impede the message that we are all one in Christ.

Often this work of reconciliation takes the form of advocating for those on the margins, and in particular the poor. As Jesus preaches in Luke 4, when we are anointed with the Spirit of the Lord, we are called to bring good news to the poor, release to the captives, sight to the blind, and freedom to the oppressed. These words are the kernel of our mission as co-workers, shaping our understanding of justice in the context of the Lord's favor—not in the context of legal systems or other ways the world constructs justice.

In other cases, the ministry of reconciliation works for healthy relationships between ethnic groups. An immigrant community from its birth, the Covenant has roots that resonate with immi-

A Commitment to the Whole Mission of the Church

grants, ethnic minorities, and multicultural communities. We have a heritage hospitable to ethnic and cultural diversity, and in recent years the Covenant has increasingly reflected the diversity of the church worldwide. Racial reconciliation is one way we embody our commitment to justice. Recalling the vision in Revelation 7, we work toward companionship with persons from all cultures and areas of the world in order to reflect the great diversity of God's people. This difficult work of reconciliation requires confession, repentance, forgiveness, and justice—all of which are key actions in Christian mission.

The ministry of reconciliation also pertains to the relationships between men and women. Throughout the world, women suffer from social, economic, and political injustices. The mission of the church includes treating women as the image of God and as fully participating members of society. Taking our example from Jesus's own life, we believe that the manner in which the whole body advocates for women, advancing their living and working conditions is crucial to the church's whole mission and to the work of reconciliation.

Amidst our ministries, we acknowledge the challenges embedded in the mission of joining together as one people and working alongside Christ. The work of reconciliation must occur on multiple levels. Yet we believe that God has called us to the work of befriending and fostering companionship across all kinds of social and cultural barriers. As part of preaching the good news, Jesus calls us to be companions who work together for justice, peace, mercy, and compassion.

A Commitment to the Whole Mission of the Church

HOLISTIC EVANGELISM

The Covenant's description of evangelism fits many of our affirmations: an insistence on biblical authority, the necessity of new birth, Christ's mandate to evangelize the world, the need for Christian formation, the responsibility for acts of benevolence, and the advancement of justice. The latter three specifically highlight the way we go about the work of evangelism holistically. The inclusion of justice and benevolence is built upon the notion that mission encompasses God's desire for Christians to follow God's heart—to make more disciples and to make the world a more caring and just place.

God calls people as partners in God's work of transformation and reconciliation in the world. As partners in this work, we are moved by our conviction that the gospel is the best possible news for all people. In this work, we are intentional about witnessing to the Christian story and engaging in the work of evangelism, partnering with groups in ways that allow for mutual growth in Christ in body, mind, and spirit.

Mission partners stand in constant need of reminders that their participation must come from the attitudes of the heart and not merely following prescribed forms. As partners in God's work, our hope lies in the transformation of people in cooperation with the Holy Spirit. Transformation refers to the concern for positive change in all dimensions of being human, including material, social, and spiritual. As co-workers with Christ we commit to a lifestyle and to choices that support life-giving ways of living for all people. Transformational work includes journeying with people in ongoing, lifelong partnerships. It is befriending, walking alongside, and being mutually formed in Christ.

Through transformational work, local communities are empowered to promote Spirit-led growth and change. When people work together, enhancing the education of children, strengthening local businesses, improving housing, and addressing their needs, the wellbeing of the community improves. In living the whole mission of the church globally, institutionally, and locally, we are challenged to offer holistic care for people in ways appropriate to their personal and cultural context, and so our work includes sustainable development, education and health care, building projects, leadership development, church planting, and other projects designed in partnership with local groups to support the flourishing of all people. Churches that were formerly mission stations are now mission sending agencies themselves, and the American Covenant is being invited back to partner in places where they were once pioneers. In so doing, we acknowledge that the flourishing of each of us is related to the flourishing of all of us.

God's mission in the world is more than a spiritual or moral influence upon society. The chosen people of God have always been called to live out their obedience in loving relationship with those with whom they live and associate (1 Peter 2:9-12). The message of a God of life was always coupled with tangible demonstrations, seen in God's community of love addressing the needs of the aliens, the strangers, the widows, the underprivileged, the poor, the blind, the needy, and the self-righteous. Covenanters understand that to partner with God in mission involves total obedience to the great commandment involving heart, soul, mind, and strength (Matthew 22:37-40).

A Commitment to the Whole Mission of the Church

The Covenant's commitment to the whole mission of the church requires a deep investment in the transforming work of God's word in the context of a healthy engagement with the world wherever Covenanters are called to serve. Out of concern that the commitment to the mission of God remains central to Covenant identity, this most recent affirmation was added in 2005 to express what had initially been central to the formation of the Covenant in the work of the Mission Friends. Although the denomination's name no longer holds the word "mission" in its title, the centrality of the commitment to the mission of the new life in Christ remains the same, even as the context of the culture in which we serve continues to change. The challenge to remain faithful in effectively living out the new life of Christ—living out the great commission and the great commandment in the changing cultural environment—is the charge to the Covenant today. Following the heart of God into the world to see more disciples in a more caring and just world—this is our mission. This is our joyful task.

NOTES

1. From the Preamble to the Constitution and Bylaws of the Evangelical Covenant Church.

FOR FURTHER READING

Anderson, Glenn P., ed. Chapters 5, 6, 7, 12, 14, 15 in *Covenant Roots: Sources and Affirmations*. 2nd ed. Chicago: Covenant Publications, 1999.

Bruckner, James. "Justice in Scripture." *Ex Auditu: An International Journal for Theological Interpretation of Scripture* 22, Justice (2006): 1–9.

Cannell, Linda. "Trying to Get It Right: Taking Seriously the Church as a People Gathered by God." *Common Ground Journal* 6 (2008): 11-20. www.commongroundjournal.org.

Chase-Ziolek, Mary. *Health, Healing, and Wholeness: Engaging Congregations in Ministries of Health.* Cleveland: Pilgrim Press, 2005.

Clifton-Soderstrom, Michelle A. *Angels, Worms, and Bogeys: The Christian Ethic of Pietism.* Eugene: Cascade Books, 2010.

Nystrom, David P. "The Covenant Commission on Christian Action." *The Covenant Quarterly* (Covenant Publications) 44, no. 3 (1987): 5-35.

Peterson, Kurt W. "Transforming the Covenant: The Emergence of Ethnic Diversity in a Swedish American Denomination." *The Covenant Quarterly* (Covenant Publications) 67, no. 1 (2009): 3-31.

Rah, Soong-Chan. *The Next Evangelicalism.* Downers Grove, IL: InterVarsity Press, 2009.

Small, Kyle J. A. "Potential for Prophetic Dialogue: Toward a Contextual Missiology for the Evangelical Covenant Church in North America." *The Covenant Quarterly* (Covenant Publications) 66, no. 3 (2008): 3-24.

Volf, Miroslav. *Exclusion and Embrace: A Theological Exploration of Identity, Otherness, and Reconciliation.* Nashville: Abingdon Press, 1996.

5

The Church as a Fellowship of Believers

HISTORICAL ROOTS

Early Covenanters frequently asked each other when meeting, "How goes your walk?" This question came naturally to those who had experienced new life in Christ and had come into a new relationship with each other in the body of Christ, the church. They understood the Christian life to be a lifelong pilgrim journey. Their life together grew into increasingly mature discipleship and service. They inquired about each other's physical and spiritual well being because they had become friends in Christ. They had committed themselves to membership in a local congregation and a denomination as formal expressions of the mystical communion of the saints—past, present, and future. Those who have found the Covenant Church to be their spiritual home have consistently responded to the call not only to believe but to *belong*.

Those who formed the Covenant Church in the late nineteenth century were by and large Swedes who for generations had been expected to conform to the norms of a state church in a kind of womb to tomb supervision. One became a member simply through birth; the requirements of baptism, confirmation, yearly communion and household examinations, marriage, and burial were enforced by law. The spiritual renewal of Pietism, beginning in the early eighteenth century, gradually embodied many forms of social protest and democratization. By the 1850s, those who had come to a personal experience of conversion as "the one thing needful" were known to each other as Mission Friends. As they formed mission societies out of their grassroots conventicles, there grew a freedom and boldness to explore the Scriptures together. They sought their own understanding of church life "as big as the New Testament itself." The relational intimacy and accountability of these small-group gatherings began to look more and more like what a local congregation should be.

Increasingly, Mission Friends on both sides of the Atlantic Ocean affirmed the biblical idea of a "believers' church." Church membership was restricted to those who could give testimony—by both their lips and their lives—that they had been befriended by Christ and had become his committed followers. They covenanted with God and each other. This process of mutual discernment and interdependence in an ongoing way called for an answer to the sincere question, "How goes your walk?" In a lecture to the World's Parliament of Religions at the Columbian Exposition (the Chicago World's Fair) in 1893, David Nyvall referred to this as the "congregational concept," the "password and ransom" of the Covenant Church, and a "conviction too strong to be silenced" by which "many may walk together."

The Church as a Fellowship of Believers

> [The local congregation] is a voluntary fellowship of spiritually alive people on the foundation of a common faith in Jesus, love, and mutual confidence; this fellowship shall be open to all who believe in Jesus and evidence this in a Christian life, independent of their doctrinal views as long as they do not contain a denial of the word and authority of the Holy Scriptures.[1]

> Our first principle is that every true believer has a right to church membership with us in all respects, and that it would be a mortal sin and treason to exclude someone who the Lord himself has received.[2]

In words attributed to Paul Peter Waldenström, membership in a fellowship of believers is like the door to the church: it should be so narrow as to exclude all those who do not witness to saving faith in Jesus Christ, but it should be so wide as to include all who do.

The Covenant Church—whether on the local, regional, or national levels—has always understood the nature of the church to be the community of the friends of Christ, mindful of his final discourse recorded in John 15. Jesus told his disciples that because of the new commandment of love he would no longer call them servants but would call them friends. Rooted in divine friendship, followers of Christ become friends to one another, who together in mission befriend others in the name of the One who first befriended them. The banner song of the renewal movement that birthed the Covenant Church began with these lines: "With God as our Friend, with his Spirit and Word, all sharing together the feast of the Lord, we face with assurance the dawn of each day and follow the Shepherd, whose voice we have heard and whose will we obey" (Carl Olof Rosenius, *The Covenant Hymnal: A Worshipbook*, #592).

There have been several cycles of planting congregations since the first four were gathered in 1868: from the new plantings of people who had been uprooted and transplanted by immigration; to the need of the second generation to form English-speaking churches; to an expanding vision of an inclusive North American church in the home mission efforts in the decades before WWII and the suburban expansion after it; to a renewed commitment to cities and their changing neighborhoods; to the planting and embrace of ethnic and multiethnic congregations and the enriching stories of people also uprooted and transplanted by immigration. In all these cycles the commitment to the church as a fellowship of believers has been a constant and unsilenced conviction.

The Mission Friend spirit has always been one of desiring harmony in the day-to-day and sometimes difficult work of walking together as congregations and in a denomination. As proclaimed in the text of the sermon by F. M. Johnson at the organizational meeting of the Covenant Church in February 1885: "I am a companion of all who fear you, of all who keep your commandments" (Psalm 119:63). So the question becomes pluralistic, "How goes our walk together?" It is an organic image, pictured in Paul's letters to the first Christian churches. The body is one but has many interdependent parts that need each other. Each is needed for the sake of extending the gospel in God's mission to the world. It is also a joyful word of welcome, which is captured in a recent Covenant hymn of gathering:

The Church as a Fellowship of Believers

Each man and woman raise your voice.
Come children sing out loud,
for everyone is welcome here
within the house of God;
for everyone is welcome here
within the house of God.

The wand'ring rebel who's lost their way,
the seeker on a quest,
both prodigal and pilgrim come
and worship in this place;
both prodigal and pilgrim come
and worship in this place.

The lonely find companionship,
the refugee a home.
Each race and culture sing as one
and all to God are known;
each race and culture sing as one
and all to God are known.

(Richard K. Carlson, *The Covenant Hymnal: A Worshipbook*, #505)

5

THE AFFIRMATION

Martin Luther, in the midst of the Reformation era, made a daring suggestion for the organization of the church:

> [Christians] should sign their names and meet alone in a house somewhere to pray, to read, to baptize, to receive the sacrament, and do other Christian works. According to this order, those who do not lead Christian lives could be known, reproved, corrected, cast out, or excommunicated, according to the rule of Christ (Matthew 18:15-17). Here one could also solicit benevolent gifts to be willingly given and distributed to the poor, according to St. Paul's example (2 Corinthians 9). Here would be no need of much and elaborate singing. Here one could set out a brief and neat order for baptism and the sacrament and center everything on the Word, prayer, and love.[3]

Luther saw the ideal church as a gathering of those who confess faith in Jesus Christ, commit themselves to each other, and submit to no authority other than Jesus Christ, the Lord of the church.

The Church as a Fellowship of Believers

The Covenant Church seeks to realize the value of this ideal.

The roots of this view of the church are found in two basic New Testament emphases:

- The church is a communion or fellowship of believers, characterized by mutual participation in and sharing of the new life in Christ. Paul calls the Christian community the body of Christ, a community composed of many members, each different and mutually interdependent (1 Corinthians 12:12-30). It is when we are in community with one another, when all of God's people are interacting with one another in worship and service, that God's will is most clearly revealed and discerned.

- The New Testament also teaches that within the Christian community there is to be neither Jew nor Greek, slave nor free, male nor female, but all are one in Christ Jesus (Galatians 3:28). These three areas—race, class, and gender—are to be of no advantage or disadvantage within the body of Christ. This is a multiethnic, classless, gender-equal vision. We recognize our need for ethnic diversity, for fellowship and mutual ministry across artificially constructed socioeconomic boundaries, and for the gifts and leadership of women and men. It is the desire of the Covenant Church to pursue this biblical vision.

The church is a gathered community set apart for involvement in Christ's mission to the world. "But you are a chosen race, a royal priesthood, a holy nation, God's own people, in order that

The Church as a Fellowship of Believers

you may proclaim the mighty acts of him who called you out of darkness into his marvelous light" (1 Peter 2:9). The "priesthood of all believers" means that every believer is called to be part of a fellowship of believers and to participate in evangelism, formation, worship, and service.

The believers' church is not simply a human institution or organization, but a people whom God has called. Emphasis does not fall on buildings or hierarchical structures, but upon a grace-filled fellowship and active participation, through the Holy Spirit, in the life and mission of Christ.

Membership in the Covenant Church is by confession of personal faith in Jesus Christ. It is open to all believers. We do not expect that all believers will agree on every detail of Christian belief. What is required is that one be born anew "into a living hope through the resurrection of Jesus Christ from the dead" (1 Peter 1:3). But if membership is open to all believers, it is also open only to believers. "The doors of the church are wide enough to admit all who believe and narrow enough to exclude those who do not," said our forebears.

This is not to claim that members of the believers' church are perfect. The church knows itself to be always a company of sinners, but sinners who have experienced forgiveness and are seeking wholeness in a new relationship to God. At the same time we affirm that all people at all stages of belief and unbelief are welcome to participate in the life of the church.

The Covenant Church believes the Holy Scriptures to be the source of the church's life, its preaching and teaching, and the means for its renewal. Jesus said, "If you continue in my word, you

The Church as a Fellowship of Believers

are truly my disciples; and you will know the truth, and the truth will make you free" (John 8:31b-32). Included in the ministry of the word is the observance of baptism and Holy Communion as sacraments of the church expressly commanded by our Lord. They are visible signs of the invisible grace of Jesus Christ. The Covenant Church is open to all believers and recognizes infant and believer baptism as biblical forms of that sacrament and includes the practice of both in its ministry.

The local congregation is of crucial importance in God's redemptive work in the world. While God is at work elsewhere, it is particularly in the close personal relationships of the fellowship that people are opened to the healing, convicting, and life-giving ministry of the Holy Spirit. Here, biblical nurture and discipline occur in the context of love and concern.

The Covenant Church is a communion of interdependent member congregations. Each local congregation seeks the guidance of the Holy Spirit in matters of common life and mission. In accordance with congregational polity, every congregation is free to govern its own affairs. At the same time, every Covenant congregation has committed itself to participate responsibly in the fellowship, decisions, and shared ministries of the regional conferences and denomination.

The Covenant Church holds that there is only one indispensable ministry—that of Jesus Christ. All members of the body are called to this ministry. It is a ministry of proclamation and evangelism, Christian formation and nurture, stewardship and servanthood. Both concern for personal salvation and for social justice are involved in the ministry. At the same time, we recognize that

The Church as a Fellowship of Believers

God calls certain men and women to be set apart as servants of the word, sacraments, and service. This does not give credentialed ministers superior status. It does recognize their call from God and gives them a special function in the church, enabling the church to fulfill its mission.

5

THEOLOGICAL REFLECTION

Church matters to God, and must matter to us as well. The church is where God is at work giving life and sharing glory (2 Corinthians 3), effecting fellowship and offering forgiveness (1 John 1), building a people of worship and witness (1 Peter 2), and building up the body of Christ into his full stature (Ephesians 4). The fourth affirmation states, "The church is not an institution, organization, or building. It is a grace-filled fellowship of believers who participate in the life and mission of Jesus Christ. It is a family of equals (Galatians 3:28)." Church is, in short, wherever new life in Christ happens.

Christians sometimes emphasize that the church is something God intended from before the foundation of the world. Luther saw Adam and Eve as the charter members of "Eden First Church," called to receive God's word of blessing and to believe God's word of promise. This line of thought demonstrates God's original intention for fellowship. God creates us for fellowship with God, with each other, and with the good creation—not as three different relationships, but as three integral dimensions of one holistic community. Until God's kingdom fully comes (Luke 22:18), church is where that fellowship is most fully realized.

Others have emphasized the church as God's measured, intentional, and saving response to human sin. Genesis 12 is the story of God, the consummate church planter, choosing Abram and Sarai to help realize a vision of a church with more members than there are stars in the sky (Genesis 15:5). This connects the church with God's redeeming love, a love prefigured and prepared in the history of Israel, fully manifested and accomplished in Jesus, and now shared in the church. God's intention for salvation has always included belonging not just to God, but to God's people. Until the new Jerusalem comes down to earth (Revelation 3:12), church is where God's salvation is most fully realized.

WE ARE A CHURCH

The affirmations begin with four declarations: *we are an apostolic, catholic, Reformation, evangelical church*. The grammar of the statement "we are a church" points out a scriptural insight about the reality of the church. The sentences are in the indicative mood, making a declaration, or a statement of fact. They are not in the imperative mood as a command. God's church exists in ways and with characteristics we can count on. It is not ultimately dependent on our hard work to make it so.

We often think of church as a community we must create or an institution we must sustain, while ignoring the fact that in Christ we already are the church (Romans 12:5). The good news is that God did all the heavy lifting while we were utterly helpless (Romans 5:8). The gospel comes to us in statements of fact: "God so loved

The Church as a Fellowship of Believers

the world" (John 3:16), "in Christ God was reconciling the world" (2 Corinthians 5:19), "the Lord has risen indeed" (Luke 24:34). The gospel does not begin with commands: "be more loving" or "stop fighting" or "don't lose hope." In Scripture such commands may follow, but the order matters: God's gift of love comes first.

Unfortunately, what we recognize about salvation—it is God's free gift—seldom gets extended to the church. Church, too, is gift before task. First Peter beautifully describes how the task of witness flows out of the gift of identity: "But you are a chosen race, a royal priesthood, a holy nation, God's own people, in order that you may proclaim the mighty acts of him who called you out of darkness into his marvelous light" (2:9). "We are church" is an announcement that being church is God's gift: "See what love the Father has given us, that we should be called children of God; and that is what we are" (1 John 3:1).

Church is where we discover our most basic, fundamental community. We can say "we" of our family, city or region, ethnic group, or country. Each of these communities may shape who we are. Yet only one of them shows and shapes our true identity as God's blessed creatures (Genesis 1:28) and beloved children (Ephesians 5:1; cf. Romans 1:7).

The church as our primary "we" matters for three reasons. Contrast Babel's "come, let *us* build ourselves a city...and let *us* make a name for ourselves" (Genesis 11:4) with Pentecost's "all of us are witnesses" (Acts 2:32). Salvation involves our exodus from communities living in rebellion against God and our entrance into the community that calls Jesus Lord (see the Barmen Declaration in *The Covenant Hymnal: A Worshipbook,* #885). There is only one community that makes us members of Christ and one another (1 Corinthians 6:15). "We are church" recounts our exodus from alienation to community, from death to life: "If we live, we live to the Lord, and if we die, we die to the Lord; so then, whether we live or whether we die, *we are the Lord's*" (Romans 14:8).

Some Christians are tempted to believe that every community—even Christ's church—is nothing more than a voluntary association of individuals. That would make church simply the sum of its parts, an aggregation of individual "I's" who choose to come together as a "we." Yet church is not just a collective noun for a group of individuals. The New Testament tells us that the church is a singular thing: "we are the temple of the living God" (2 Corinthians 6:16), and "we are [Christ's] house" (Hebrews 3:6), and most explicitly, "we, who are many, are one body in Christ, and individually we are members one of another" (Romans 12:5). Just as your body is more than an amalgamation of its parts, so Christ's church is more than a group of individuals.

When Christians say "we," they include their Christian brothers and sisters around the world. Christians' churchly identity is more important than their civic or any other identity. Church is our primary community, because "Christian" is our primary identity. Our calling is to live for our one Lord, by our one faith, in our one baptism (Ephesians 4:1-5). Locally, Covenanters take the specific time and place of their "we" very seriously. They devote themselves to small group discipleship, acts of mercy, and faithful membership and worship in local churches.

CHURCH IS WHERE THE ACTION IS

The Evangelical Covenant Church affirms the church as a fellowship of believers. To understand this phrase, we look at the three key nouns: church, fellowship, and believers. But we also look for some related strong verbs along the way, because church is where the action is.

The New Testament word for church is *ekklesia*, a noun created from the verb *to call*. The word does not stand alone, as the New Testament typically speaks of the church of God. Paul writes "to the church of God that is in Corinth" (1 Corinthians 1:2; 2 Corinthians 1:1), and speaks elsewhere of the church as God's (1 Corinthians 10:32; 11:22; 15:9; Galatians 1:13; 1 Timothy 3:5, 15). "Church" has a theological meaning precisely because it is always *God's* church. Its members are active in ministry, because God is active in them.

The affirmation speaks of a "believers' church" rather than of "God's church," not in contradiction, but because the believers' church is "a people whom God has called," not simply "a human institution or organization." We are sometimes prone to think that we bring forth the church by our own striving—by our steadfast prayers, or faithful serving, or regular attendance, or cheerful giving. Of course, our worship, work, and witness are all necessary, but they are necessarily a response to what God is already doing—creating the church. It is because of this reality that believers are empowered to struggle in hope within local churches in broken communities through prayer, witness, service, and discipleship.

It is no accident that the verb form of *ekklesia* means "to call together" or "to call into assembly." The word invites us to ask,

"Who called this meeting?" and to answer resoundingly, "God did!" It is the church of God because God called it into existence, God called it out of captivity into freedom (Exodus 20:2), God called it from death to life (Romans 6:13), God called it out of darkness into God's marvelous light (1 Peter 2:9). It is God's church because of God's calling; it exists by the will and action of God. "God is faithful; by him you were called into the fellowship of his Son, Jesus Christ our Lord" (1 Corinthians 1:9). It is a believers' church, because it is God who has created us, called us, and formed our belief.

After Peter's confession of faith, Jesus says, "On this rock I will build my church" (Matthew 16:18; 1 Peter 2:5). We might be tempted to think that Peter's faith came first, and thereby made it possible for Jesus to build a church. But note how God's initiative precedes and produces Peter's faith: "Blessed are you, Simon son of Jonah! For flesh and blood has not revealed this to you, but my Father in heaven" (Matthew 16:17). Indeed, faith is God's gift to us, because "at its deepest level [faith] depends upon the mysterious yet gracious action of God."[4] Church is not created by our efforts, or even by our faith. God creates the church just as surely as God created the heavens and the earth (Ephesians 2:15; 3:9; Colossians 1:16; 2 Corinthians 5:17; Galatians 6:15).

Paul's key body passage in 1 Corinthians 12:12-13 makes this clear, because in it the passive verbs show that we are the objects of God's activity. We were all baptized and we were all made to drink of one Spirit. As God's project, the church is neither subject to our control, nor finally vulnerable to our failures. It is God at work in Christ who will finally present the church without spot or wrinkle

(Ephesians 5:27). In this confident hope, we are the church—across generations, praying through sickness and trouble, offering forgiveness in confessed failure, struggling to understand Scripture in small group Bible studies, visiting the sick and imprisoned, and teaching children the way of God.

God has given the church key practices through which divine life is given to the church. The affirmation mentions preaching and teaching, and the observance of baptism and Holy Communion. Sometimes we group these four practices as the ministries of word and sacrament. But here we can treat sacraments as performance and embodiment of the scriptural word of promise. Communion is a ministry of the word—breaking bread together with glad and generous hearts (Acts 2:46) in obedience to Jesus's command to "do this in remembrance of me" (Luke 22:19; Matthew 26:26-29; Mark 14:22-25), thereby proclaiming "the Lord's death until he comes" (1 Corinthians 11:26). More broadly, two communion prayers in *The Covenant Hymnal: A Worshipbook* recount the scriptural story from creation to consummation, helping us to see that we celebrate this meal not by looking back at Scripture, but by dwelling within it.[5]

Baptism, too, is a ministry of the word: washing persons (1 Corinthians 6:11) in obedience to Jesus's command to "go make disciples...baptizing" (Matthew 28:19-20), a proclamation of our incorporation into Christ's death and resurrection (Romans 6:4; Colossians 2:12). Where other denominations have allowed divergent views on baptism to fuel division in the church, the Covenant has sought to remain united around "one Lord, one faith, one baptism" (Ephesians 4:5), even while recognizing that Covenanters hold diverse views about baptism. Therefore, the Covenant Church "recognizes infant and believer baptism as biblical forms of that sacrament and includes the practice of both in its ministry." Again *The Covenant Hymnal: A Worshipbook* contains prayers that set our performance of baptism within the larger scriptural story of God's creating and redeeming work.[6]

Word and sacraments are not the only scriptural practices by which God enlivens the church. "Singing and making melody to the Lord" (Ephesians 5:19) is a key ministry of the word in congregational worship. God uses sung Scripture to nurture and strengthen our faith. Not every song is equally faithful to the scriptural story, and some focus too much on the individual believer and too little on God. Our music, like our preaching, teaching, and practice of the sacraments, must remain subject to Scripture, "the only perfect rule for faith, doctrine and conduct."

FELLOWSHIP: IS IT NOT A SHARING IN CHRIST?

The second key noun in this affirmation is *fellowship,* an English translation of the Greek term *koinonia.* The Pauline benediction in 2 Corinthians 13:13 prays that "the grace of the Lord Jesus Christ, the love of God, and the communion [fellowship/sharing] in the Holy Spirit be with you all." The Trinitarian shape of this blessing can help us see that our fellowship in the church is far more than our warm feelings toward one another. It is our participation in the intimate personal relations of the Father, Son, and Holy Spirit. The church father Cyprian understood this when he said church is "the people united by the unity of the Father and the Son and the Holy Spirit."

The Church as a Fellowship of Believers

The Covenant's historical strength is in the face-to-face fellowship of participation in small gatherings of believers. Here the work of struggling in prayer together, engaging the Scripture, and building one another up in Christ is accomplished. The affirmation describes this fellowship as "grace-filled" and suggests that it entails "close personal relationships." That ordering is important, for fellowship is God's gift rather than simply our task. Sometimes Christians talk as if fellowship is a quality of relationship—or even a feeling of affection—that we can and must produce by our own efforts. Fellowship becomes *koinonia* when it is enlivened by the Holy Spirit. In 1 John 1:3, our fellowship with one another is not something different from our fellowship with the Triune God. They are two dimensions of one complex fellowship. Christ's incarnation was not only about new life but also new fellowship (1 John 1:1-4).

The fellowship of small gatherings is not something additional to our salvation, but simply the complex relational dimension of that new life. The New Testament makes it clear that anyone who has God as Father belongs thereby to "a large family" (Romans 8:29), the very "household of God" (1 Timothy 3:15). Jesus certainly had this communion of relationships in mind when he taught us to pray "our Father" rather than "my Father" (Matthew 6:9). We cannot have fellowship with Jesus and not with our brothers and sisters. The gift of new life in Christ is both fellowship with God and fellowship with God's people. Membership in a local congregation has been a standard for Covenanters from the beginning.

Fellowship with one another in the presence of God is precisely what our celebrations of baptism and Holy Communion enact. So Paul, who affirms that "all of us who have been baptized into Christ Jesus" (Romans 6:3), also affirms that "we were all baptized into one body" (1 Corinthians 12:13). Baptism enacts our participation not only in Christ, but also in each other. This newborn child of God is also our brother or sister in Christ. There is a story from the early history of the Covenant in which a pastor refused to continue the tradition of changing the water in the baptismal font between baptisms of peasants and gentry. Here was a lived enactment of the bold claim that in Christ there is neither slave nor free (Galatians 3:28). Baptism both receives a *koinonia* already given in Christ, and seeks to enact and embody it.

Likewise with communion: Paul writes, "the bread that we break, is it not a *koinonia* in the body of Christ? Because there is one bread, we who are many are one body, for we all partake of the one bread" (1 Corinthians 10:16b-17). Communion enacts not only our dependence on Christ, but also our mutual interdependence. One cannot do communion alone, because properly we share the elements with one another as together we share in Christ.

Sharing this meal together as Christ's church serves as an enactment of Jesus's inclusive table fellowship. Jesus lived at a time when people were concerned to eat with the right kind of people. To eat together implied friendship and equality. So who did Jesus eat with? Jesus ate with the rich and the powerful, with the poor and the needy, with well-known religious leaders and with well-known sinners, with men and women, in short, with just about anyone. Because he did not limit his dining to the right people, Jesus had a reputation for eating with the wrong sort of people, so he was called a "glutton and a drunkard, a friend of tax collectors and sinners" (Matthew 11:19).

Jesus's disciples have since been identified not only as those who eat with him, but also as those who eat like him. We eat like him when many races, ethnicities, the rich, the poor, the young, the old, women, and men gather as equals at the one fellowship table of Christ. The table is where the "one new humanity" in Christ ought to be most visible (Ephesians 2:15).

Fellowship is a gift we receive. Once that is established, we can recognize that it is also a task for us to embody more and more faithfully. The challenge might be political viewpoints, ethnicity, musical tastes, social class, generational divides, or factions in the church. Whatever the particulars, every church can find encouragement in the logic of Paul's first letter to Corinth. Writing to a congregation deeply divided into factions, a church whose communion table enacted division rather than sharing, Paul lays out the logic of *koinonia* as the gift that leads to task: "God is faithful; by him you were called into the fellowship (*koinonia*) of his Son, Jesus Christ our Lord. Now I appeal to you, brothers and sisters, by the name of our Lord Jesus Christ, that all of you be in agreement and that there be no divisions among you, but that you be united in the same mind and the same purpose" (1 Corinthians 1:9-10).

A PRIESTHOOD OF BELIEVERS

The final key noun in this affirmation is *believers*. The church is comprised of believers, that is, of persons who confess faith in Jesus Christ as Lord. Historically Covenanters insisted on personal faith because nonbelievers were included as members in the state church in Sweden. They commonly asked one another, "Are you alive yet in Jesus?" and "How goes your walk?" Yet they did not

The Church as a Fellowship of Believers

presume that their personal faith was the foundation of the church. They recognized that faith is the effect of God's working (Philippians 2:13) and the gift of God's grace (Ephesians 2:8). This faith has personal content, but it is a relationship—a relationship of trust in and allegiance to the Lord Jesus Christ. Thus faith is deeply personal, but it is never private.

Covenanters have an organically personal, rather than institutional, understanding of the body of Christ. They assume actual human and familial bonds between believers commonly known as a "family of faith." This includes acts of kindness, loyalty to one another, forbearance, and humility in conversation and relationships, even where some hierarchical structure is in place. Covenanters also generally expect believers to be present in worship, to tithe their income, and to develop personal relations with other believers. Small group gatherings are taken seriously as a means of prayer support and personal growth in Christ.

How believers get along matters to Covenanters. Historically we have been described as "warm Pietists" rather than cold legalists. We care about our relational life together and our growth in the grace of Christ. To this end we encourage and mutually seek evidence of growth in personal faith and integrity in relationships. Covenanters assume that believers will display evidence of the Holy Spirit and the gospel of Christ as active forces in improving their behavior toward others. We live out our justification through Christ in terms of fellowship with one another.

There are two helpful ways for thinking about how our believing relates to the church. The first is to consider our new birth by grace through faith: "Are you alive yet in Jesus?" The New Tes-

The Church as a Fellowship of Believers

tament makes it clear that the new birth relocates us. This relocation can be described as moving from death to life, from darkness to light, from old to new. Most centrally, the new birth incorporates us in Jesus Christ. Faith is, as stated in the affirmation, "a grace-filled fellowship and active participation, through the Holy Spirit, in the life and mission of Christ."

Believers are alive in Christ (1 Corinthians 1:30) which means that they are Christ's church (Romans 16:16; Galatians 1:22) and that they are Christ's body (1 Corinthians 12:12-27; Ephesians 1:22-23; Colossians 1:24; 1 Corinthians 10:16-17; 11:23-30). For this reason, the old Covenant adage that "the doors of the church are wide enough to admit all who believe and narrow enough to exclude those who do not" needs to be carefully interpreted. It does not mean that there are some believers outside Christ's church. What the old saying must mean is that formal entrance into the institutional church is restricted to believers; *only* believers in Christ are welcome to join the institutional church, but also that *any* believer is welcome. In addition, unbelievers are warmly welcomed to seek Jesus in the midst of the congregation, to hear the gospel clearly articulated, and to experience the saving love of God in Christ.

The second way our believing relates to church follows Matthew 18:20, where Jesus promises, "Where two or three are gathered in my name, I am there among them." To gather in Jesus's name is to gather as those who confess with their lips that Jesus is Lord and believe in their heart that God raised him from the dead (Romans 10:9). As a result, as stated in the affirmation, "membership in the Covenant Church is by confession of personal faith in Jesus Christ." This promise also shapes congregational worship, as confessing our faith plays a crucial role in the life of the church. We do not merely listen passively to Scripture and preaching, but we speak our faith in corporate confessions and personal testimonies, we sing our faith in robust hymns and rich songs, we pray our faith silently and aloud.

The verses surrounding Matthew 18:20 define the practice of forgiveness by which the church lives. A believers' church is not a sinless community but a fellowship of sinners saved by grace through faith. Therefore, forgiveness is an essential practice by which God creates and sustains the church. Sin happens, and when it does Christ intends for his church to continue his reconciling work, seeking to redeem the sinner and restore fellowship. Sin is not merely a private problem between the sinner and God.

In Matthew 18:22, Jesus directs the church to forgive seventy-seven times, overwhelming the logic of retribution with a superabundance of forgiving grace. Jesus's point is not that there is a limit to the number of times that we are to forgive one another, but that the cycle of violence that Cain started and Lamech escalated (Genesis 4:24)—a cycle that leaves us all bleeding and estranged—must be replaced by a cycle of escalating forgiveness. Living that way is only possible in the light of the resurrection and in the power of the Holy Spirit. The first thing the risen Christ does in John's Gospel is impart the Holy Spirit and empower the church to forgive (John 20:22-23). The church lives as a community of forgiveness precisely because it "knows itself to be always a company of sinners," yet a company whose companion is the forgiving Lord. As a people, the church embodies the replacement of human hostilities with divine peace (Ephesians 2:14-18).

The Covenant affirms that believers have a priestly calling by using the Reformation phrase "priesthood of all believers" (1 Peter 2:9). God has called the church to bear the world to God in prayer, and to bear God to the world in faithful witness and loving service. It is a priestly office that claims the whole church in its total life. The church as a whole shares in Israel's vocation to be a light to the nations (Isaiah 42:6; Matthew 5:14). Lesslie Newbigin expounds this theme, "The whole core of biblical history is the story of the calling of a visible community to be God's own people, His royal priesthood on earth, the bearer of His light to the nations."[7] Before the church can have an adequate notion of the priesthood of each believer, it must embrace the prior notion of the priesthood of the entire church for the sake of the world.

Within that priestly office each believer also finds a role. Each believer is gifted by the Spirit for the good of the whole church (1 Corinthians 12:7). So in exercising their gifts, each believer is participating in the one ministry of Jesus Christ, our great high priest (Hebrews 4:14-15). To affirm the priesthood of all believers is to imagine the ceaseless circulation of gifts among members of the body for the edification of each and the up-building of all. The heart of the matter is found in those passages that speak of Spirit-given gifts that build up the church (Romans 12:4-8; 1 Corinthians 12:1-11; Ephesians 4:8-16). These passages do not offer an exhaustive listing of spiritual gifts, nor a detailed description of the gifts mentioned.[8] Instead, they guide us to the source, the purpose and the extent of gifting. God gives spiritual gifts by the Holy Spirit, and the Spirit ever remains the source of their effectiveness. Gifts are not identical with natural aptitude, lived experience, nor

The Church as a Fellowship of Believers

acquired skill. They depend on the Spirit, who distributes them "according to his will" (Hebrews 2:4; 1 Corinthians 12:11). Spiritual gifts are given for the "the common good" (1 Corinthians 12:7); that is, their purpose is the total health of the body of Christ (Ephesians 4:12b-13).

When the Reformers affirmed the priesthood of all believers, they were trying to free the church from captivity by clergy. Calvin taught that every Christian is his or her own priest, not needing a pastor or anyone else to connect with God. This way of putting things could come to mean that we do not really need our fellow Christians in the church or that "I can be Christian all by myself." Luther, however, insisted that we always need someone else to tell us the good news about Jesus. True, our faith is in God, a personal relationship with the Father in the Son by the power of the Holy Spirit. But our faith comes by hearing the gospel spoken to us by a brother or sister in Christ (Romans 10:14). Every Christian can be a priest to fellow believers, saying, "I can be your priest, and you can be mine."

A church committed to the priesthood of all believers places a responsibility on every member to participate actively in the total life of the church, to bear witness to the gospel in word and deed, to "serve one another with whatever gift each of you has received" (1 Peter 4:10), and to receive the service of another's gifts. The church is not comprised of two groups—ministers who offer ministry, and laity who receive it. The affirmation states that the church has "only one indispensable ministry—that of Jesus Christ. All members of the body are called to this ministry." Thus, every member is *minister* and every member (even a pastor) is *ministered to*.

Every member of the body is called both to give and receive ministry, and it damages the body just as much when laity fail to do ministry as when clergy fail to receive it.

Affirming that all are priests does not mean, however, that none should be pastors. The Covenant holds that "God calls certain men and women to be set apart as servants of the word, sacraments, and service." In doing this, the Covenant recognizes the New Testament emphasis on God's calling and gifting of particular persons for particular ministries, and to that end, we wholeheartedly ordain both women and men to the profession of pastor. According to the measure of Christ's gift, "some would be apostles, some prophets, some evangelists, some pastors and teachers" (Ephesians 4:11). Where some traditions have searched the New Testament for an exact template of ministerial office, the Covenant has found there a flexibility of form. Covenant theologian Donald Frisk spoke for the church when he wrote, "We are persuaded that the Holy Spirit continues to create new forms of ministry to meet new situations."[9] From time to time the Covenant has *reordered* credentialed ministry, but it has never failed to *order* it for the good of the whole church. The point of this ordering is not power or prestige for pastors, but that the church may be built up into the full stature of Christ (Ephesians 4:12-13).

Finally, we must emphasize that the church is a pilgrim people on their way to the ends of the earth with the good news of the gospel and to the end of time when we shall meet our Lord. "Until Christ comes, we will continue to worship, work, and witness...."[10]

The Church as a Fellowship of Believers

NOTES

1. Glenn P. Anderson, ed., *Covenant Roots: Sources and Affirmations* (Chicago: Covenant Press, 1980), 163.

2. Ibid., 168.

3. Ulrich S. Leopold, ed., *Liturgy and Hymns* (Philadelphia: Fortress Press, 1965), 53.

4. Donald C. Frisk, *Covenant Affirmations: This We Believe* (Chicago: Covenant Press, 1981), 7.

5. *The Covenant Hymnal: A Worshipbook*, 943, 945.

6. Ibid., 932, 934.

7. Lesslie Newbigin, *The Household of God: Lectures on the Nature of the Church* (New York: Friendship Press, 1954; reissued, Eugene, OR: Wipf and Stock Publishers, 2009), 20

8. Frisk, 164-68.

9. Ibid., 167.

10. *Covenant Affirmations*, rev. ed. (Chicago: Covenant Publications, 2005), 21.

FOR FURTHER READING

The Covenant Book of Worship. Chicago: Covenant Publications, 2003.

Frisk, Donald C. "The Church and Sacraments" and "Mission and Ministry." Chaps. 9 and 11 in *Covenant Affirmations: This We Believe*. Chicago: Covenant Press, 1981.

Lohfink, Gerhard. *Does God Need the Church?* Collegeville, MN: Liturgical Press, 1999.

Newbigin, Lesslie. *The Household of God: Lectures on the Nature of the Church*. New York: Friendship Press, 1954; reissued, Eugene, OR: Wipf and Stock Publishers, 2009.

Phelan, John E. Jr. *All God's People: An Exploration of the Call of Women to Pastoral Ministry.* Chicago: Covenant Publications, 2005.

Weborg, C. John. "Pietism: A Question of Meaning and Vocation." *The Covenant Quarterly* 41, no. 3 (1983): 59-71.

6

A Conscious Dependence on the Holy Spirit

HISTORICAL ROOTS

"Are you still living in Jesus?" What did early Covenanters mean when they asked this question of each other, and how might such a living and growing faith even be possible? Several generations of young people in the Covenant Church—donned in white confirmation robes symbolizing baptism, with much committed to memory—have recited the following words of explanation to the third article of the Apostles' Creed on sanctification:

> I believe that I cannot by my own reason or strength believe in Jesus Christ, my Lord, or come to him. But the Holy Spirit has called me by the Gospel, enlightened me with his gifts, sanctified me and kept me in true faith, even as he calls, gathers, enlightens, and sanctifies the whole Christian Church on earth and keeps it with Jesus Christ in the one true faith. In this Christian Church he

daily and abundantly forgives all my sins, and the sins of all believers, and will at the last day raise me and all the dead, and will grant eternal life to me and to all who believe in Christ. This is most certainly true.[1]

One would be hard-pressed to find a more succinct statement concerning the mystery of faith that is believed, hoped, and made one's own in love, as well as what sustains it on a daily basis within the believing community of the church. Conscious dependence on the Holy Spirit is both a divine gift and a human necessity.

John Bunyan, the seventeenth-century English Puritan pastor who wrote the classic spiritual allegory *The Pilgrim's Progress*, said, "Examples speak more powerfully than precepts." The story of Covenant pioneer pastor Carl Magnus Youngquist unites in a compelling fashion an example of the Holy Spirit's sustaining presence in the life of an individual with the organically integrated structures of the church and its people, all united by one Spirit. Born in 1851 into poverty in southern Sweden, an area known as "the Swedish Jerusalem" because of widespread revivals, young Carl met Jesus at the age of eight in Miss Storckenfelt's Sunday-school class, an educational model imported from the United States. He later remembered, "She was a lady of rank and culture, and the aristocracy always filled me with terror." That quickly changed, however. The leveling affects of the renewal movement—in this case that of the social classes—may be seen to have been the work of the Spirit among persons of faith.

As mass emigration intensified, Youngquist boarded the train in Jönköping, which finally would take him to Gothenburg and the waiting ship that would carry him to North America. He was eighteen and alone, yet there were so many fellow pilgrims that they filled sixty-five passenger cars pulled by two steam locomotives. At twenty-two, he was one of the first ministerial students at the school begun by Mission Friends in Keokuk, Iowa. Youngquist soon became a pioneer Covenant pastor planting and serving several congregations, a founding delegate of the Covenant Church in 1885, and the fledgling denomination's first historian. He was an able writer with a keen sense of the history unfolding about him, and while in Nebraska he began to record the earliest narratives while editor of the monthly *Hem-Missionären* (The Home Missionary).

In 1899, C. M. Youngquist was called to the Covenant congregation in the gently rolling farm country of Lund, Wisconsin, not far from the broad widening of the Mississippi River known as Lake Pepin. The little church was already celebrating its twenty-fifth anniversary. Typical of his generation of pastors and their know-how, he often worked alongside the farmers in their fields, especially during the long, demanding days of planting and harvesting. Sometime in 1900, Youngquist scratched his leg on a rusty barbed-wire fence. He thought little of it until the infection worsened, leading to blood poisoning and tetanus, and ultimately to gangrene—now spread to both legs. He was seriously ill and expert medical care was needed should his life be spared. It is here that the extended beloved community of a young denomination may be seen, consciously dependent on the presence of the Holy Spirit. Pastor Youngquist could have gone to the nearby twin cities of Minneapolis and St. Paul with their fine hospitals. But no, he wanted to go to Chicago where the Home of Mercy and Swedish Covenant Hospital were located, to be near so many of his longtime spiritual friends.

Now an invalid with an escalating fever, Youngquist was placed on the train for Chicago in Red Wing, Minnesota. His final pastoral act in Lund occurred when the youth of his confirmation class, who had come to the station, boarded his car one by one for conversation and words of encouragement, prayer, and blessing. There were tears, as well, as those so full of young life suspected that they were also bidding farewell to their pastor.

After several days, on August 10, 1901, the decision was made to amputate both legs in an attempt to stem the spread of infection. As he was being prepped for surgery, surrounded by Covenant leaders, Youngquist called for the seminary students and faculty in nearby North Park to walk the few blocks to the hospital, also to receive his words of encouragement and blessing. Then, as he was wheeled into the operating theater, Youngquist began to sing the final verse of a familiar hymn by Carl Olof Rosenius: "Pierced heart, with love o'erflowing, guide me, help me through life's desert find my way; let my faith, no matter what betide me, find assurance in your wounds each day. To your presence—for this life is fleeting—take me, wash my garments in your blood; and with Thomas may I, at your meeting, cry with joy, 'My Lord and God!'" (*The Covenant Hymnal: A Worshipbook*, #427). No doubt, other voices joined his. Youngquist passed away during the surgery, "still living in Jesus."

It is impossible to know, of course, what may have been in the minds and hearts of those young people the following May on confirmation day at the mission house in Lund, with its lovely graveyard next to the simple, white-clad church building where several Covenant pioneers and pastors were already resting, awaiting the "great and glorious day of Christ, our Lord."[2] One surmises, however, that their thoughts also held close the blessed memory of Pastor Youngquist and his nurturing of their lives, perhaps as they recited from memory Luther's explanation to the third article of the Apostles' Creed.

A spiritual song, written by Swedish Covenant itinerant evangelist and pastor Joel Blomqvist (1840-1930), echoes the ancient ninth-century Latin hymn, *Veni Creator Spiritus* (Come Creator Spirit):

> Heav'nly Spirit, gentle Spirit,
> O descend on us, we pray;
> come, console us and control us,
> Christ most fair to us portray.
>
> Hear us pleading, interceding,
> O interpreter of love;
> with your fire—us inspire,
> holy flame from God above.
>
> Pilgrims, strangers, 'mid life's dangers,
> we on you would e'er depend;
> Spirit tender, our defender,
> guide us, keep us to the end.
>
> (*The Covenant Hymnal: A Worshipbook*, #287)

6

THE AFFIRMATION

The Covenant Church, rooted in historic Christianity, affirms one God as Father, Son, and Holy Spirit. The Holy Spirit continues the creative work of the Father and the redeeming work of the Son within the life of the church. It is for this reason the Covenant Church has emphasized the continuing work of the Spirit.

According to the Gospel of John, the earthly Jesus promised that the same Spirit of God that "remained on him" (1:32) would one day live in his disciples as a result of his crucifixion and resurrection. The Spirit "abides with you," he said, "and will be in you" (14:17). It was this Holy Spirit that came to abide in Paul, filling him with the presence of God and directing him, just as it had Jesus. For this reason Paul could claim, "it is no longer I who live, but it is Christ who lives in me" (Galatians 2:20). It is the Spirit in us that enables us to continue Christ's mission in the world (Acts 1:8).

The New Testament affirms that the Holy Spirit works both within and among individuals. It is the Holy Spirit that draws together those who are far off and estranged, causing them to be made one in Christ (Ephesians 2:11-22). It is the Holy Spirit that stirs within each of us a deep sense of familial affection for one another, so that we are beloved to one another (1 Corinthians 15:58). It is because Christ has become our brother (Romans 8:29) that we are together members of the family of God (Ephesians 3:14-16). It is the Spirit of God within us that cries "Abba," as we have been adopted into the family of God, sisters and brothers one with another (Galatians 4:4-7). It is the Holy Spirit, Paul asserted, that affords a sense of unity and common purpose among Christians (Philippians 1:27; 2:1-2).

The Covenant understanding of the Holy Spirit, rooted in the New Testament, is further informed by the Reformation idea that word and Spirit are inseparable. It is the Spirit of God that enlivens the preaching of the gospel within the community of faith and grants efficacy to the sacraments participated in by the community of faith. The Covenant also draws upon its Pietist heritage for understanding the Holy Spirit. We believe it is the work of the Holy Spirit to instill in the human heart a desire to turn to Christ. We believe it is the work of the Holy Spirit to assure believers that Christ dwells within them. We believe that the Holy Spirit, in concert with our obedience, conforms us to the image of Christ (Romans 8:28-29).

The early Covenanters in Sweden were linked by a common awareness of the grace of God in their lives. They spoke of the Holy Spirit communicating this warm sense of God's grace to each one individually and directing them to a common devotion to God in Christ through the reading of the Bible and frequent meetings for the purpose of mutual encouragement and edification. They perceived the Holy Spirit leading them corporately to common mission

A Conscious Dependence on the Holy Spirit

and purpose.

The early Covenanters in North America were conscious of the presence and purpose of God through the activity of the Holy Spirit among them. They were certain the Holy Spirit was at work in their churches and particularly in leading them to form the Swedish Evangelical Mission Covenant denomination. At the organizational meeting of the Covenant, C. A. Björk spoke to the effect that an organizational meeting can never produce unity; God's people become one, he said, through the leading of the Holy Spirit. The early Covenanters believed that each Christian needs to await the voice of God as revealed not only to the individual, but also through the witness of other believers. They believed the Holy Spirit is alive and active, working through preaching, the sacraments, the Scriptures, and in the witness of one another.

The Covenant Church believes that the Spirit of God is active and "blows where it chooses" (John 3:8). The Spirit is the prevenient actor in the drama of salvation, the creator of hunger for Christ's life, and the fulfiller of that hunger. We are often surprised at the unfolding of God's purpose, suggesting that our ways and thoughts are not always the ways and thoughts of God. For this reason Covenanters desire to cultivate a healthy humility before God open to the leading of the Holy Spirit. When God is about doing a new thing, we wish to perceive God at work rather than be found dull to the divine purpose. We wish to see with the eyes of the Spirit, and not merely with our own. The Covenant Church believes with Paul that the Holy Spirit endows believers with spiritual gifts, the purpose of which is to serve the Christian community that is the very body of Christ. As a believer's church the Covenant has valued the Reformation concept of the priesthood of all believers, and sees it rooted in the idea of mutual interdependence expressed in Paul's notion of the body (1 Corinthians 12:12-31). The Spirit bestows gifts on individual Christians for the benefit of others, not the benefit of the one who has received the gift. It is the plan of God through the work of the Spirit that within the body of Christ we need one another. Accordingly, while recognizing the legitimacy of all the spiritual gifts, the Covenant Church has historically been unmarked by an emphasis on any one or one type of spiritual gift. This deep trust in the gentle leading of the Spirit has remained true of the Covenant Church through the years.

6

THEOLOGICAL REFLECTION

That the Covenant Church in a relatively short list of affirmations focuses one exclusively on the third person of the Trinity is, in itself, worthy of note. It helps us remember what sometimes is forgotten. In the Christian West, with the possible exception of communions or movements within Wesleyan, Pentecostal, or charismatic heritage, focus on the Holy Spirit both in thought and practice is often blurred.

One reason for this neglect, ironically, is that the Holy Spirit is so pervasively present in almost every aspect of Christian experience. Though not always mentioned, the presence and power of the Holy Spirit is at work in all six Covenant affirmations. As with ministries of evangelism and stewardship, if everything has to do with either, it is likely that witnessing and giving will be taken for granted and seldom faithfully done. So with the Holy Spirit—essential but often assumed or conflated into the work of the Father and the Son. Covenant theologian Donald Frisk finds a second reason in "the eschatological nature of the work of the Holy Spirit.... Because his work is not yet completed, a certain unfinished quality

A Conscious Dependence on the Holy Spirit

is inevitable in all our utterances concerning his ministry."[3] Historian Richard Lovelace points to a third reason in what he calls "the sanctification gap."[4] Lovelace documents how strong affirmation of the work of the Holy Spirit in the theology of Reformation churches and their descendants experienced steady decline and neglect from the eighteenth century onward, not only in theological emphasis but in ecclesial practice. The central role of the Spirit becomes sidelined perhaps for fear of behavioral extremes of persons "taken up with the Spirit."

Despite the Covenant's strong affirmation on the Holy Spirit, the danger of neglect is always present for the Covenant as for any church. Nevertheless, the fifth affirmation has remained central to the Covenant's faith, life, and work and to its exposition we now turn. Following sections on the scope of what "conscious dependence" might mean, and why broader reference to the Holy Trinity needs be part of the discussion, we will focus on presence (who the Holy Spirit is) and power (what the Holy Spirit does) as a dual fulcrum for what life in the Spirit is all about.

CONSCIOUS DEPENDENCE

An affirmation of conscious dependence pushes us to consider a wide range of relationships between subject and object. Paradoxically, such spectrum reaches from total control to total surrender. On one end is the case of Simon Magus, a sorcerer who was introduced in Acts 8. Even though his "magic" made him great in the eyes of the people of Samaria, the witness of the disciple Philip was even greater, and Simon was one of many who came to believe in Jesus (Acts 8:9-13). But for Simon, even his own baptism was not enough. Seeing the power of the Holy Spirit come upon others when Peter and John "laid hands on them," Simon tried to purchase such power for himself by means of money (Acts 8:17-19). Peter rebuked him for such an attempt to control. Since then throughout the course of church history any attempt to purchase, guarantee, or control the Holy Spirit has been known as the practiced heresy of "simony." Likewise, any claim on the Holy Spirit based on what we have given through right action, right belief, right disposition, or right offering is not really depending on the Holy Spirit but expecting what one wants and is due.

As an example, consider the Spirit's presence and work when the sacraments of the church are enacted. Even though right words in a liturgical setting are important, they are no guarantee that the Holy Spirit will show up in presence and power at human utterance. At Holy Communion, it is important for the pastor, priest, or presider to pray the *epiclesis,* the prayer of consecration asking for the Holy Spirit's presence in and through the elements before they are given to the recipients for their forgiveness, healing, and growth in grace. Without such petition to the Divine, the table is but a centerpiece in a nice human drama. But even when "everything is ready," the faithful regularly return to the table knowing that they are asked for faithful action without guarantee of special blessing. The Spirit will come in God's time, through God's means, because of God's promise (Matthew 18:20) and not through human deed, voice, or wish.

At the other end of the spectrum of what conscious dependence might mean is a trust in God so complete that it is beyond conscious will itself. It is a trust that minds not because it matters

A Conscious Dependence on the Holy Spirit

not. This position is clearly beyond what the Covenant Church intends by its use of the word *conscious*. What we affirm is surely a radical trust in the disposition and activity of the Triune God toward humankind, but it is a trust that is willed and chosen. This trust is not a mindless, non-caring, "whatever." Rather it is a trust that we embrace because we are assured that God embraces humankind and will purpose well for whatever circumstances we experience. It is not only the "blessed assurance" of the gospel hymn that "Jesus is mine," but also the confident affirmation of the prophet: "Do not fear, for I have redeemed you; I have called you by name, you are mine." Even if life's path must pass through flood and fire, "you are precious in my sight, and honored, and I love you" (Isaiah 43:1, 4a).

Sometimes affirmations are better sung than said. At the core of every Covenant hymnal in English from 1931 to the present is the hymn "How Firm a Foundation." While not exclusively centered on the third person of the Trinity, it is about the Triune God and what is promised the believer who consciously depends.

ASPECTS OF THE TRINITY

The Covenant is often mistakenly characterized as a "non-creedal" church. It is true that the Covenant does not have a "confessional" statement at the heart of its theological identity. It has no Augsburg (Lutheran) Confession, no (Presbyterian) Confession of 1967 or Westminster Confession of 1648, no (Roman Catholic) Baltimore Catechism, no articles of faith that are doctrinally inviolate and imperative for the consent of the believers. Instead it has the "affirmations," which are some "central beliefs" beyond the two most basic: confession of Jesus Christ as Savior and Lord and acceptance of the Bible as the word of God.

So, really, the Covenant is a "non-confessional" church that does use some creeds as occasional parts of its worship. Such creeds are presented in *The Covenant Hymnal: A Worshipbook*. They include many scriptural passages, are written in many languages, and are drawn from the broad Christian heritage. They include the Apostles' Creed and the Nicene Creed (with additions by the Council of Constantinople, AD 381). Both basic creeds are distinctly Trinitarian.

The Trinity is a complex doctrine. It is hard to explain how one God can be in three persons. As such, it is a major barrier to dialogue among the monotheistic Abrahamic faiths, including Judaism and Islam. Some suggest that it is not a biblical doctrine, as it is mentioned only as part of a baptismal rite (Matthew 28:19). Yet it is basic to the common faith of the Covenant Church and includes the person of the Holy Spirit as part of that Trinity. For purposes here only three aspects of this doctrine will be discussed: sovereignty, mutuality, and language.

Sovereignty. Human want, desire, and need to control are ever in tension with a sovereign God who will do as God so chooses. God's call and incorporation of all who turn and believe are not always welcome to others. The Ogden Nash tongue-in-cheek poem, "How odd of God to choose the Jews," is but a smirk on the angry face of Christians ever resentful of the Jewish peoples. That the genealogy of Jesus (Matthew 1:1-16) includes women is an affront to a male-dominated culture. Even more repulsive, the five women included are a rejected conniving harlot, a prostitute, a foreign refugee, an adulteress, and an unwed pregnant teenager. Yet God chose these women for God's purposes.

One of those purposes, the incarnation of God's Son, finds such persons soundly judged and criticized for associating with the wrong kind of people, especially sinners (Matthew 11:19 and following). This Son describes the third person of the Trinity as the "wind" that "blows where it chooses, and you hear the sound of it, but you do not know where it comes from or where it goes" (John 3:8a). In short, the Triune God is sovereign, free to choose. And so God acts, in Father, Son, and Holy Spirit. To forget that, or to think otherwise because of a self-affirming freedom apart from God, is to act only as flesh, and to walk thereby and not in the Spirit (Matthew 26:41, Ephesians 2:3, and Galatians 6:8).

The fourth Gospel in itself provides strong witness that the inner relationships between Father, Son, and Spirit (advocate, counselor) as *persons* of the Trinity are not of necessity connected to the needs and wants of humankind. That the trinitarian God acts toward and on behalf of humankind is a grace and not a given. Sovereignty implies difference, even separation. The biblical witness testifies that the separation between a sovereign God and the creation is bridged by a God who loves so much that God *is* love (1 John 4:16 and throughout the letter). Contemporary colloquial Christian apologist, Anne Lamott, puts it this way: "God loves us exactly the way we are, and God loves us too much to let us stay like this."[5] Thus the love of God involves the Spirit's work in sanctification, or growing in grace.

Mutuality. Even though the subject of the inner workings of the Trinity is seldom a central focus of contemporary theology, that issue was a major area of speculation in the developing doctrine of early Christianity. One of the terms used to describe the internal relationships between and among the Father, Son, and Holy Spirit was *perichoresis*, "dancing around together." Such an anthropomorphic, almost folksy, description of the three-personed God has, because of its Greek linguistic technicality, become lost for common Christian thought. It need not be. Its quaint image of the inner life of God pictures for humankind what communal life might look like if the Trinity is at all a model for our life together.

Most people have some mental picture of what Jesus looks like. Covenanter Warner Sallman's *Head of Christ* painting has, since the 1940s, been normative for a wide swath of evangelical Christians in the West. Likewise, spiritual directors can recount the multiple images of God the Father that run through the cognitive lenses of those who seek their listening ear. But of the life of the Holy Spirit there is little image save for the wind, seen only in its effect, not in itself, and the dove, where emphasis is placed on the descending, not on the companion itself.

The image of "dancing around together" offers a trinitarian model for human existence. Life is fundamentally relational. Dancing is disciplined *and* free, ordered *and* expressive. To consciously depend on the Holy Spirit is not only duty but delight. And perhaps most importantly, it is done together. The early church, in its discernment of God's direction, did not depend on a single voice, but on what "seemed good to the Holy Spirit and to us" (Acts 15:28). A church business meeting can be more than an agenda and decisions. It can be a dance. Process can be as important as product. How we treat each other as persons can be as important as outcomes.

This picture of communal life should not be hard for Covenanters to understand. From our tentative beginnings we have known that the venture ahead is not just about "my God and I." What the Spirit is about is an "us" thing. Note the title of our primary communal autobiography by Karl A. Olsson, *By One Spirit*. Surely Covenanters have written theology individually in books and artifacts, but like this book it is done *en famille*, in concert, with others. So also the mission conference recorded in Acts 15 shows that big issues are given to communal discernment, not singular authority ("it seemed good to the Holy Spirit and to *us*"). Similarly, from the beginning, our mission activities have surely involved heroic saints and cadres of supportive colleagues and congregations. More recently, our worldwide missional activity focuses on partnership. In short, we do not dance alone.

Language. In many languages, nouns and verbs naturally dominate as descriptors of actors and actions. But other parts of speech have their own subtle power to change meaning, direction, and consequence. For example, consider the range of difference between a congregation's "ministry *to* youth" and a "ministry *through* youth." A simple prepositional change alters everything, including purpose, how persons are perceived, what pronouns are employed, and the nature of human community itself. John Calvin's description of the Holy Spirit was "God at work in, through, and among us." Full elaboration of these three prepositions not only point to a wide range of activity, but when yoked together they guard against heresy in thought or deed. Heresy always tends to take a part for the whole. For example, God at work only within and not through and among, focuses on my blessing, growth, and gifting, ignoring

A Conscious Dependence on the Holy Spirit

social purpose or communal realities.

Therefore, to depend on the Holy Spirit is to embrace an endless vista of activity as life unfolds and the Spirit leads. The Christian does not know where, to whom, for what end, or why the Holy Spirit might lead. Consider Philip in Acts 8:26-40. Depending on the Spirit, all Philip did was trust and obey; all that resulted was God's glory and neighbor's good. Calvin's propositions "in, through, and among" are a good starting place. But include as well "with, beside, beyond, above, below, before, behind, after, in front, for, against, within, without, on, at." Dependence on the Holy Spirit may on one day provide comfort *in* a rough place. The next day the Spirit may lead one *out of* a comfort zone *into* a rough place.

A second linguistic issue has to do with pronouns. Because the third person of the Trinity is variously named in a gender mix (the Spirit, *ruach,* of God in Hebrew is feminine; in New Testament Greek the Spirit, *pneuma,* is neuter; and in church Latin the *Spiritus* is masculine), pronounal confusion has been consequence. Until recently men have usually controlled both liturgical and theological language about God, so the Spirit of God is commonly he, him, or the impersonal "it." Resolution of the matter is beyond present purpose save for a plea for more imagination in the use of inclusive language and a reminder that it is "God in three *persons,* blessed Trinity" of whom we sing and praise. As Pietists, our faith is a personal matter with a personal God. A neutered force is not enough.

THE HOLY SPIRIT AS PRESENCE

Many, if not most, of us Christians have found ourselves in situations where we are at the end of our resources and crying out

A Conscious Dependence on the Holy Spirit

in desperation for the Spirit of God to come to our aid. The early Christians desert fathers and mothers commonly prayed Psalm 70:1 as part of life's experience: "Be pleased, O God, to deliver me. O Lord, make haste to help me!" It is as if we are alone and God is away. But the promise of the One who sends us into the work of the kingdom breaks through any aloneness and comforts with the words, "And remember I am with you always" (Matthew 28:20b). The presence of God's Spirit is not an accidental happenstance. It is a promise sure. It is as close as our breathing.

We don't usually focus on our breathing until something—high altitude, lung disease, or even the common cold—interferes with it. We assume it as a matter of course. But in the beginning it was God's breath that caused life to be (Genesis 2:7). In the valley of dry bones, bone, sinew, and flesh came together, but there was no life until the breath of God was given (Ezekiel 37:8-10). So also with the disciples, hiding in fear until Jesus breathed the Spirit upon them (John 20:22). The Nicene Creed reads thus: "We believe in the Holy Spirit, the Lord, the giver of life" (*The Covenant Hymnal: A Worshipbook*, #883). How many times a day does one affirm this? With each breath is the rhythm of inhale and exhale. With such, life begins; by such, life is sustained; without such, life is gone. Such is the presence of God's Spirit.

Yet, how many of us regularly rest in the presence? Is the discipleship mandate so strong to be purpose-driven that simply being present to the Spirit of God is an afterthought? Are action and achievement more important than attending and listening? I often make lists of things to do. When have I listed or listened who to be? At the beginning of creation the Spirit of God was hovering over the watery chaos (Genesis 1:2). The same Spirit still hovers over the chaos we make of our lives. Always present. Ever with peace.

For humankind resting is not an option. Like breathing, like eating and drinking, certain functions and activities are essential to life. The created is ever made with limits. That's what the garden story is all about (Genesis 2-3). And the human story is ever about limit breaking. Who hasn't "pulled an all-nighter" to get a paper done or to prepare for a test? Who hasn't pledged to "not rest until this is over"? Who hasn't ignored the fourth commandment because one's own work takes priority over God's rest? Who hasn't suffered ill consequence because of all of the above? Built into creation and the human body are limits that might be challenged and tested, and that advancing science might promise to overcome, but they remain in some form. Should there ever come a political state where taxes do not exist, people will still die.

As important as the myriad of actions of the Holy Spirit are in keeping life alive and full, growing and glad and giving, the presence of the Spirit provides a rest amidst the rush, a calm amidst the problematic. The Holy Spirit provides human response to the divine command: "Be still, and know that I am God!" (Psalm 46:10). An old familiar hymn affirms that "there is a place of quiet rest near to the heart of God" (*The Covenant Hymnal: A Worshipbook*, #85). Its chorus names Jesus as the provider of such a place, but it is the dancing together trio that is fully at work. Together in concert they will to be so present to the human busy brain and body that one can know a peace that passes understanding (Philippians 4:7).

In some earlier theological debates, the nature of "assurance" focused exclusively on whether or not the believer knew that he or she was really "saved," or if such status was yet conditional and dependent on whatever. What the Covenant Church affirms by a "conscious dependence on the Holy Spirit" worries not about previous assurance issues. Instead it embraces an assurance that in whatever circumstance we find ourselves, there is a promised rest, a confidence of companionship, a foundation that will remain firm, and a calm that fear can threaten but not destroy.

Such assurance allows one to go to sleep when rest is needed. It allows one to welcome the world upon arising. It steadies amidst confusion and soothes when troubles come. Even if there are not controllable guarantees about life in the Spirit, there are promises. Conscious dependence both holds onto them and is held by them. "For the Son of God, Jesus Christ…was not 'Yes and No'; but in him it is always 'Yes.' For in him every one of God's promises is a 'Yes'" (2 Corinthians 1:19-20). Perhaps we need another "blessed assurance" hymn that rests in the Spirit's promise: "As a mother comforts her child, so I will comfort you" (Isaiah 66:13).

THE HOLY SPIRIT AS POWER

As much as we might be less mindful of the significance of the Spirit's presence, we are fascinated by the Spirit's power. Or we are wary of those who claim to have it. My paternal grandfather, an early Covenant pastor, smiled when he spoke of *Missionsvänner,* "Mission Friends," but almost spit when referring to *Pingtsvänner,* "Spirit Friends." Among churches seeking that which is "done decently and in order" (1 Corinthians 14:40) or social legitimacy in a larger culture, the Spirit's demonstrable powers are often toned down. Nonetheless, we deeply value how God's Spirit is at work among us. We follow with brief consideration of where, what, and how such happens.

Where. To assert that the Holy Spirit is at work everywhere may be true but such claim "forks no lightening," as Dylan Thomas put it. Formative power demands particularity. Hence Jesus of Nazareth is sent by God, not an idea of global goodness. Locations for the Holy Spirit's powerful work have already been mentioned in regard to the sacraments, the believer's heart, mind, and actions, and the church's discernment and decision. Especially important for the Covenant Church, we include as well the Spirit's formation of an ecclesial body, the understanding and interpretation of Scripture, the pre-conditional activity for the ministry of evangelism and mission, and the efficacy of preaching.

Because the pulpit has had such prominence in the Covenant Church, the role of the Holy Spirit in preaching demands much more attention than space permits here. Fundamentally the church has believed that whatever occurs in the hearer's heart and conscience from listening to a sermon is more the result of the work of the Spirit than the preacher's skill, knowledge, or rhetorical devices. Akin to the preaching issue is the church's worship as a whole and the revival service in particular. The tension here regarding the Spirit's presence and role is easily over a century old. For some, orchestration is the mandate. Like Finney's early nineteenth-century revivals, worship must be "worked up." For others, like his contemporary New England colleagues, revival is to be "prayed down." The Holy Spirit may well be present in both and equally depended upon, but in different ways.

There is a certain irony that Karl Barth, often critiqued for his overdependence on revelation, is most insightful on this point. Barth himself does not completely disdain learning from other human sciences. In fact he points out that God commanded the soon-to-be-freed Israelites to take whatever riches they could from the Egyptians for potential use (Exodus 11:2-3 and 12:35-36). That various kinds of silver and gold may be found in other, even alien, treasures is not the issue. That Charles Finney's use of certain techniques improved revival's success is not the issue either. Dependence on prayer alone may be praiseworthy, but it does not mean that all other resources are employed in vain. At issue is whether or not the other resources eventually become a golden calf, worshiped in place of God (Exodus 32:1-35).

Another issue of location for the Holy Spirit involves not only place but time. Both the Son and the Spirit are in time: the former was born in Bethlehem, nurtured in Nazareth, crucified and raised in Jerusalem. And the latter was breathed upon the disciples (John 20:22) and filled the faithful at Pentecost (Acts 2:1-4). Yet both are beyond time as well. Christ is at and before creation (John 1:1-13; Colossians 1:15-17) and the Spirit is active over a formless void before creation (Genesis 1:1-2). An affirmation of conscious dependence is only buttressed by Scripture's witness to power within and beyond time.

Because some confirmation materials, lectionaries, and strict followers of the church year inadvertently isolate the role of the Holy Spirit to Acts 2, it is important to underscore the time-encompassing work of the Spirit. God's Spirit is not limited to a day in Jerusalem with the appearance of indigenous languages, tongues of fire, a memorable sermon by Peter, and 3,000 saved. Surely this was remarkable and well described as "the birthday of the church." But it does not describe the abundance of the power and presence of the Spirit. In fact, often lost among the day's wonders are two socially significant factors in the text. That people heard the message in their own language (Acts 2:8) prefigures God's contextual mission strategy, and Peter's use of the Joel 2 text bears witness to a gospel that will turn the social order upside down (Acts 2:17-21).

Many have witnessed to two other loci where the Holy Spirit is present and active: in the individual unconscious and in the very public rites of the laying on of hands in acts of ordination and consecration to special ministries. The Bible is replete with God's communicating through dreams, even if many scoff at them or dismisses their significance. The laying on of hands is equally biblical and involves a communication of some kind of power beyond our knowing. As a form of blessing and sign of empowerment, it makes sense. Beyond that, not.

Since Cyprian's declaration in the third century that outside the church there is no salvation, there has been a tendency within Christendom to locate the presence and power of the Holy Spirit within ecclesial boundaries or at least adjacent to them. Christian thought has become more open to the possibilities that the work of the Spirit is not church bound. The issue is really a very old and technical one beginning with the Western church's addition of the *filioque* clause ("and the Son") to the creed in AD 589 (*The Covenant Hymnal: A Worshipbook,* #883) regarding God's sending of the Spirit and its process of progression through the Father and the Son. More to the point for purposes here is the practical reality that the church has replaced *filioque* ("and the Son") with *eccleseique* ("and the church") and contended against any possible consideration that there may be some Spirit-occasioned salvific work outside the missions of the church itself: "The church does not have a mission; the mission has a church."[6]

This is not to suggest that any and all manifestations of spiritual happenings are those of the Holy Spirit. We are instructed by 1 John 4:1-3 to "test the spirits." They need not be church-bound, but they should be Christ-bound. In other words, the Holy Spirit's activity may have no immediate connection with the province and/or control of the church, but it should in some way point to Christ. Here is one reason why the Western church added the *filioque* clause ("and the Son") to the creed. And perhaps it is a more contemporary reason why many new "converts" across the globe refer to themselves, not as "Christians," but as "followers of Christ."

What. Beyond issues of where the Spirit is at work are the kinds of work the Spirit does. As noted earlier, the activity of the Holy Spirit is so rich as to include almost everything connected with Christian experience. But to say all is to say nothing. Therefore clustered in eight categories below are a series of participles that attempt to encompass the range of the Holy Spirit's work in the lives of individuals, groups, and institutions alike.

Attached to each category are but a few selected biblical texts as illustrative witness. Also included for each category are hymns or songs from Covenant hymnals. Such are listed because the Covenant Church has always been a singing church. For many of the faithful, when exact words do not come immediately to mind, a tune might bring to awareness an assurance of spiritual presence or a memory of spiritual significance. As noted earlier, some truths are

A Conscious Dependence on the Holy Spirit

simply better sung than stated. And as Royce Eckhardt, Covenant hymnologist, has often claimed: "It matters not whether you can sing, but only if you have a song."

Even if the Scripture texts are common for all of us, the use of hymns is not to suggest that such are normative. Such simply point to heritage. Contemporary music equally is illustrative of the Spirit's work.

1) *Inspiring, edifying, reviving, renewing, stirring* (Isaiah 61:1-3; Ezekiel 37:9; Joel 2:28-29; Romans 15:30; 1 Corinthians 2:9-11). As a member of an African American congregation I regularly hear a prayer of thanksgiving for "waking me up this morning." For many folks, life is hard and an extra boost sometimes needed, even to get out of bed. So we are grateful when the very breath of the Spirit of God shows up as in "Breathe on me, breath of God, fill me with life anew, that I may love whate'er you love, and do what you would do" (*The Covenant Hymnal: A Worshipbook*, #283).

2) *Guiding, leading, directing, turning* (Psalm 143:10; Zechariah 4:6; John 4:23-24; Acts 8:29; Galatians 5:16-18). In a world increasingly filled with options and choices, sorry is the soul that must decide everything on his or her own without solid guidance. Even beyond the counsel of friends and family, the Holy Spirit's promptings remain a promised compass for the Christian pilgrim. As the hymn, "Holy Spirit, Faithful Guide" claims: "Ever present, truest Friend, ever near Thine aid to lend, leave us not to doubt and fear, grasping on in darkness drear" (*The Hymnal* [1950], #210).

3) *Judging, convicting, changing, discomforting* (Isaiah 40:7, 13; 63:10; 1 Corinthians 3:16; 2 Corinthians 3:17; Revelation 2:1–

A Conscious Dependence on the Holy Spirit

3:22). True friends are those who can say "no" as well as "yes," those who can challenge as well as comfort, correct as well as confirm. In the hymn "Spirit of God, Descend upon My Heart," we testify to this aspect of the Spirit's work in us: "Teach me to feel that you are always nigh; teach me the struggles of the soul to bear, to check the rising doubt, the rebel sigh; teach me the patience of unanswered prayer" (*The Covenant Hymnal: A Worshipbook*, #294).

4) *Gathering, unifying, reconciling* (Isaiah 34:16; Acts 15:28; 1 Corinthians 12:4-7; Ephesians 4:3-6; Revelation 22:17). Despite our Pietist heritage, which sometimes can become so individually focused that we lose sight that we are an "us" and not just a "me," the heritage hymn, "O Breath of Life," reminds us that God's Spirit is who makes us one, keeps us one, builds us together, and empowers our common witness and service: "O Breath of life, come sweeping through us, revive your church with life and pow'r: O Breath of life, come, cleanse, renew us, and fit your church to meet this hour" (*The Covenant Hymnal: A Worshipbook*, #599).

5) *Growing, nurturing, conforming, building* (Judges 13:24-25; John 3:5; John 14:16-17; 2 Corinthians 3:3, 17-18; Galatians 3:5; 5:22-25). As mentioned earlier, God loves us wherever we are found and loves us so much as not to leave us there. The hymn "Holy Ghost, with Light Divine" echoes this and underscores the Reformation doctrine of sanctification. Surely justified by the grace that is in Christ Jesus, we are ever being sanctified, growing in the grace given by the Holy Spirit: "Holy Spirit, all divine, dwell within this heart of mine; cast down ev'ry idol throne, reign supreme and reign alone" (*The Covenant Hymnal* [1973], #267).

6) *Interceding, voice-giving, encouraging* (Numbers 27:18;

A Conscious Dependence on the Holy Spirit

Micah 3:8; Romans 8:26-27; 1 Corinthians 12:3; Galatians 4:6; Ephesians 6:18). Even our voiced prayers are the Spirit's work, and the fruit of our work in the world depends on the Spirit. This truth is affirmed in the nineteenth-century hymn "Christians, We Have Met to Worship" in a new stanza that was first introduced in 1990 in the Covenant songbook *The Song Goes On*: "May the Spirit's interceding move our hearts with ev'ry prayer, help us follow where you're leading, keep us in your tender care. Lord we go now from this gath'ring, strength renewed with hearts aright, to the world where you have called us; send us forth as salt and light" (*The Covenant Hymnal: A Worshipbook*, #502).

7) **Comforting, assuring** (Job 27:3-4; Psalm 139:7; Luke 11:13; 1 Corinthians 6:11; 2 Corinthians 1:22; 5:5). Neither God the Father nor Jesus the Son make false promises. In the presence and power of the Holy Spirit, the comforter has come. The hymn "Heavenly Spirit, Gentle Spirit," quoted earlier in this chapter, has another verse: "Come to cheer us, be thou near us, kindle in us heaven's love; keep us burning, humble, yearning, dwell in us, O heavenly Dove." (*The Covenant Hymnal* [1973], #269).

8) **Creating and recreating** (Genesis 1:2, 2:7; Job 33:4; Psalm 104:30; Revelation 11:11). The song is short; the text (Psalm 51:10-13) is direct; the meaning of "Create in Me a Clean Heart," is clear. Without the Spirit our own spirits become forfeited: "Cast me not away from your presence, and take not your Holy Spirit from me. Restore to me the joy of your salvation, and uphold me with a willing spirit" (*The Covenant Hymnal: A Worshipbook*, #360).

Thus said or sung, in text or tune, there is ample witness to the work of the Holy Spirit to underscore the Covenant's affirmation of "conscious dependence." Over or exclusive focus on the multiple activities of the Holy Spirit may tempt one to forget that the Holy Spirit is the third *person* of the Trinity, not the third *function* of God.

Moreover, it is important to underscore that in affirming the range of the Spirit's activities and the scope of all the Spirit's gifts, the Covenant is careful not to make any one particularly normative for Christian experience. Thus we are not a "charismatic denomination" yet we are fully open to the Spirit's benevolent sovereignty in a Christian's life and the Christian church.

How. The ways that the Holy Spirit accomplishes work are as multiple as the works themselves. But Scripture provides humankind with two broad categories for the Spirit's instrumentation: fruit and gifts.

1) *Fruit.* The nine fruits of the Spirit that Paul lists in his letter to the churches in Galatia (5:22-23a), are dispositions, qualities, or characteristics of persons or groups who are "led by the Spirit" and "live by the Spirit" (5:18, 25). These fruits are love, joy, peace, patience, kindness, goodness, faithfulness, gentleness, and self-control. (The NRSV translation substitutes "generosity" for goodness, a reading debated by New Testament scholars.)

Paul's choice of fruit as metaphor is ingenious, almost an acid test of what "conscious dependence" is really about. One does not will fruit. Fruit requires preparing soil, planting, nurturing, pruning, and receiving harvest at ripeness—but not before or later. The Spirit's fruit is far different from a New Year's resolution. Surely conscious work is entailed in both, but the latter one succeeds only through self-will. The other comes by God's will and in God's time and in God's way. One wants; the other waits. One plans and accomplishes; the other trusts and receives, recognizes and gives thanks.

2) **Gifts.** The gifts of the Spirit are identified in several New Testament passages, primarily Romans 12:6-8; 1 Corinthians 12:1-11; Ephesians 4:7, 11-12; 1 Peter 4:10-11. The Christian disciple can explore as well the narratives of the Hebrew Bible and Acts to identify where the *ruach* or Spirit of God rests on the faithful, thus gaining a broader vision of how the Spirit supports, sustains, judges, or transforms humankind or particular individuals. These actions are also "gifts," even if they are not immediately perceived as such. When they come is not of one's own agency. A harsh learning may be labeled a judgment, but it may also be a gift.

There are several on-going issues about the gifts of the Spirit. These include whether they are only canonical or can, like "hospitality," be affirmed in the present. There are always issues surrounding extraordinary gifts like healing and prophecy and the means of discerning gifts. It seems clear that the gifts of the Spirit are given for building up the church (1 Corinthians 12:7; 14:4-5, 12), but the lines between individual giftedness and corporate well-being are not always clear.

An even larger issue is often obscured by debates about the gifts of the Spirit. Lost in this contention is that the sending of Son and Spirit is not because God loves the church, but the world (John 3:16). God's yearning is as much, if not more, for those without the church as for those within. Gifts are given to be shared, or at least to equip those consciously willing to share. Gifts are not so much to be possessed as to be passed on, for love's opposite is not hate but selfishness. Holding on, rather than letting go, is to misunderstand and misuse the Spirit's gifts altogether. Letting go into God's hands that with which we are blessed with a conscious dependence on the Holy Spirit is God's plan and purpose for all Christian disciples.

CONCLUSION

Even though we can sing with gusto from Luther's hymn "A Mighty Fortress" that "the Spirit and the gifts are ours," many of the Spirit's gifts sit around the church unopened and hence unused. Such is so for many reasons: a lack of awareness of God's resources or a lack of trust in them; theologies that confine such gifts to other times, special circumstances, or saintly persons; convictions that rule out what might not fit our present program; or church leaders uninterested in taking the time to find out what gifts might be present in the people of their congregations.

Perhaps that is why God has over time had to remind, recall, renew, and revive both Israel and the church that what is missing is not the power and presence of the Spirit, but our own awareness and confidence in such person. The rise and reality of persons and movements in church history such as the Montanists, the monastics, the mystics, the Wesleyans, Pentecostals, and charismatics may well be God's way of having the third person of the Trinity blow through the door to awake those of us relaxing in comfortable pews. Most recently, the renewal and growth of the Christian church through Spirit movements in Africa, Asia, and Latin America may challenge western theological and practiced conventions, and offer fresh options for a revived faith.

Ever present and powerful is the Holy Spirit. Poured out, the

Spirit will gift the young with prophesy and visions; the old shall yet dream of what is to come, and on those of societal lower degree shall come power. The wonders of heaven shall appear on earth and deliverance shall gift those who seek even to survive (cf. Joel 2:28 ff). And for those of us who primarily seek simply presence, God's shepherding Spirit will provide "a settled rest...no more a stranger, or a guest, but like a child at home" (*The Covenant Hymnal: A Worshipbook*, #91).

NOTES

1. Martin Luther, *The Small Catechism*, 1529

2. A. L. Skoog, "We Wait for a Great and Glorious Day," *The Covenant Hymnal: A Worshipbook* (Chicago: Covenant Publications, 1996), 772.

3. Donald C. Frisk, *Covenant Affirmations: This We Believe* (Chicago: Covenant Press, 1981), 108.

4. Richard F. Lovelace, "The Sanctification Gap: Articulating the Christian Experience," *Theology Today*, 29/4 (January, 1973): 363-69.

5. Anne Lamott, *Traveling Mercies: Some Thoughts on Faith* (New York: Pantheon Books, 1999), 135.

6. Joseph A. Grassi, "Blueprint for a Missionary Church: Scriptural Reflections on the Church as People of God," in *The Church as Sign*, ed. William Jerome Richardson (Maryknoll, NY: Maryknoll, 1968), 16.

FOR FURTHER READING

Frisk, Donald C. "The Holy Spirit and Salvation." Chap. 8 in *Covenant Affirmations: This We Believe*. Chicago: Covenant Press, 1981.

Frisk, Donald C. *The New Life in Christ*. Chicago: Covenant Press, 1969.

Heron, Alasdair I. C. *The Holy Spirit*. Philadelphia: Westminster Press, 1983.

Johnston, Robert K, ed. "The Ministry of the Holy Spirit in the Covenant

Today." *The Covenant Quarterly* (Covenant Publications) 44, no. 4 (1987): 49-53.

Lovelace, Richard F. "The Sanctification Gap: Articulating the Christian Experience," *Theology Today* 29, no. 4 (January 1973): 363-69; later included as Chap. 7 in *Dynamics of the Spiritual Life*. Downers Grove, IL: InterVarsity Press, 1979.

Olsson, Karl A. *By One Spirit*. Chicago: Covenant Press, 1962.

7

The Reality of Freedom in Christ

HISTORICAL ROOTS

In *Concept of Anxiety,* nineteenth-century Danish philosopher and theologian Søren Kierkegaard wrote that bondage to sin is fundamentally rooted in the reality of human freedom. Humanity is created in the image of God with the unique freedom to choose and, Kierkegaard claimed, anxiety is the precondition and consequence of humanity's having chosen poorly, with the absolute inability to will the eternal good among all the possibilities faced by each person. We are justified by grace through faith, and only the saving work of God in Christ restores true liberty. The anxiety inherent in being finitely human before the infinite Creator is a universal human experience that runs deep. Confronting the reality of anxiousness in the face of human freedom and finitude, early Covenanters spoke and sang freely about anxiety. They did so because they had experienced new life in Christ. They had experienced the reality of true freedom in Jesus, and while life still held worries, that kind of deep anxiety was no longer to be feared.

Nils Frykman (1842-1911) began one of his many songs with the question, "Why should I be anxious?" Immensely popular in Mission Friend gatherings and Covenant life, the composition of words and joyful tune was the result of a specific personal crisis. Frykman had been a school teacher long before he became a Covenant pastor in Sweden and then in the United States, following his emigration in 1886. The sweeping educational reform act of 1842 had created new schools in Sweden to train professional teachers; the instruction of children had previously been entrusted solely to pastors, with wide degrees of effectiveness. Since the movement of spiritual renewal was closely aligned with social reform and personal initiative, many Mission Friends sensed a call to the vocation of teaching. It was inevitable that they were often accused of proselytizing beyond the formal religious instruction prescribed by the state.

Though mindful of professional boundaries, Frykman experienced intense scrutiny and the accusations of parents and civil authorities. Summoned once again to appear before the school board, he became paralyzed in anguish. On the way to the meeting, he stopped his horse and buggy and fell to his knees in despair, weeping and crying out to God. Gradually he was infused with peace and assurance, and with new confidence he resumed the journey to face his accusers. Prior to his arrival at the school, he had already sketched in his mind the words and music: "Why should I be anxious? I have such a Friend, who bears in his heart all my woe; this Friend is the Savior, on him I depend, his love is eternal, I know" (*The Covenant Hymnal: A Worshipbook*, #431). He sang these words, and he was free.

Several key biblical passages were discussed prior to the unanimous vote by delegates gathered in Chicago in February 1885 to form the Evangelical Covenant Church. Among them was Galatians 5: "For freedom Christ has set us free. Stand firm, therefore, and do not submit again to a yoke of slavery" (v. 1). Having experienced liberating new life in Christ, Mission Friends had turned their attention to discussions about the communal and ecclesial dimensions of freedom, and were now prepared to shape the identity of a new denomination. An example of this is an open view that accepted both infant and believer's baptism as biblically and theologically grounded. A difficult tension to live with at times because it granted freedom of discernment to individuals and families apart from doctrinal prescription, the Covenant's stance on baptism was rooted in discussions during the 1870s and emerged with clear conviction. If we believed that the Lord desired all the children of God to be together, then surely baptism should not be a doctrine that divided those who had experienced the reality of freedom in Christ—as sadly it had for 450 years. The history of baptism in the Covenant Church, therefore, has been an important litmus test in its understanding of theological freedom with a communal commitment to the Bible's authority standing above any individual interpretation.

It is readily apparent that the Covenant affirmation on the reality of freedom in Christ is inseparable from the affirmation on the centrality of the Scriptures. Early Covenanters believed that the most important consequence of the atonement controversy was that it led the majority of Mission Friends to a unified clarity about the nature of the church and a generous orthodoxy of doctrinal freedom apart from official creeds and confessions. This freedom, however, was condemned as dangerous by the Lutheran State Church in Sweden and its counterpart in the United States, the Augustana Synod. A critical and symbolic moment occurred ten years before the Covenant Church was formed in Chicago. The "Galesburg Rule" was adopted in 1875 by the annual conference of Augustana in an effort to control the "Waldenströmians," thought to be devouring the immigrant landscape like grasshoppers because of their critique of the Augsburg Confession. When the rule stated that only credentialed Lutheran pastors were allowed to preach in Lutheran pulpits, and only credentialed Lutheran members allowed to receive communion, the Mission Friends replied: "The pulpits for all evangelical preachers and the Lord's Table for all the children of God." This too was a declaration of freedom in Christ. The invitation to communion in the Covenant Church states, "All who put their faith and trust in Christ are welcome at this table."

The architects of the early Covenant Church, twice-born in their experience, possessed a mature ideal of not only what constitutes the church, but how individuals may harmoniously live together with humility and integrity. Though it has often remained an ideal into which one strives to live, Covenanters affirm that freedom is much more that which is granted to others than claimed for oneself. David Nyvall called it the last of the spiritual gifts to mature, to be free for the sake of others even more than self.

Nils Frykman began his spiritual song literally in Swedish with the words, "Why should I cry?" A committed Christian, like many he still suffered occasional bouts of anxiety and melancholy. An authority on Swedish Covenant hymns said that Frykman's au-

The Reality of Freedom in Christ

thentic joy and freedom in Christ also served to drive out the darkness. So with him, in another of his hymns, the believer proclaims:

> I sing with joy and gladness,
> my soul has found release;
> now free from sin and sadness,
> with God I live in peace:
> his everlasting mercy
> to me has been revealed,
> his truth in my heart has been sealed.
>
> Now marching on courageous,
> with joy I see my goal:
> the blessing of the ages,
> the haven of my soul:
> and on the pilgrim journey
> my voice in song I raise,
> my God and my Savior to praise.
>
> (*The Covenant Hymnal: A Worshipbook*, #498)

7

THE AFFIRMATION

The Covenant Church seeks to focus on what unites followers of Jesus Christ rather than what separates them. The center of our commitment is a clear faith in Jesus Christ. The centrality of the word of God, the necessity of the new birth, a commitment to the whole mission of the church, the church as a fellowship of believers, and a conscious dependence of the Holy Spirit form the parameters in which freedom is experienced. Here followers of Christ find the security to offer freedom to one another on issues that might otherwise divide.

Freedom is a frequently misunderstood concept. In western culture freedom is often understood as autonomy and independence. No one, however, can truly be autonomous and independent. Authentic freedom manifests itself in a right relationship with God and others. It is for this reason that freedom in Christ is so highly valued in the Covenant Church. Freedom is a gift of God in Christ to all who are willing to receive it. "If you continue in my word," said Jesus, "you will know the truth, and the truth will make you free" (John 8:31b-32).

The Reality of Freedom in Christ

Liberation is one of the Bible's major themes. Early in their story, God's people were liberated as slaves from Egypt and began their long journey to the promised land. The story continues with the liberating work of the judges, who delivered Israel from its enemies. Israel's greatest king, David, liberated them from the Philistines and established a kingdom committed to Israel's God. But this kingdom did not stand. The Hebrew Scriptures end with Israel once again in bondage to their enemies, but living with the promise of God's deliverance. Throughout this story the freedom of God's people is not just freedom from, but freedom to. They are set free from Egypt to worship and serve their God. In their law they are called not only to serve one another, but the stranger, the alien, the widow, and the orphan—all who suffer and are marginalized by the bitter circumstances of life.

Jesus came as God's anointed one to continue God's program of liberation. He sets us free, according to Paul, from the power of sin to condemn, control, and destroy. God's people are not without sin, but find in Jesus's death and resurrection the glorious liberty of the children of God. But, as in the Hebrew Scriptures, this freedom is never simply personal and individualistic. By the power of his life-giving Spirit, Christ moves us into a new realm—a new kingdom where light and life and joy prevail. "For freedom Christ has set us free" (Galatians 5:1a). Thus empowered, the believer not only seeks to obey and follow God, but to effect the liberation of others from the sins and oppressions of their lives. This freedom is "in Christ." By grace God makes a person, with Luther, "a perfectly free lord of all, subject to none" and at the same time "a perfectly dutiful servant of all, subject to all." For Paul such freedom means believers are set free from the binding restrictions of culture and creed to live into a new reality: "There is no longer Jew or Greek, there is no longer slave or free, there is no longer male and female; for all of you are one in Christ Jesus" (Galatians 3:28).

True freedom is found in this creative tension between the "lordly" and servantlike spirit. God wants individuals to be who and what they were created to be in perfect freedom. This freedom is not for self-indulgence but to serve the community and the world out of love for God (Galatians 5:13).

The Covenant Church has sought to honor the tensions inherent in this freedom. The Covenant Church has understood that God's word is sovereign over every human interpretation of it—including its own. Covenant freedom operates within the context set by other principles the Covenant Church regards as primary, particularly the authority of Scripture. Within these parameters the principle of freedom applies to doctrinal issues that might tend to divide. With a modesty born of confidence in God, Covenanters have offered to one another theological and personal freedom where the biblical and historical record seems to allow for a variety of interpretations of the will and purposes of God. This has at times led to controversy over such matters as baptism, the second coming of Christ, the precise nature of inspiration or how the atonement may be understood, and various matters of life and practice. Nevertheless, commitments to the Bible as the word of God and the historical interpretative consensus of the Christian Church have remained a constant. This commitment to freedom has kept the Covenant Church together when it would have been easier to break fellowship and further divide Christ's body.

The Reality of Freedom in Christ

To some such freedom is no freedom at all. They would rather have the marching orders clear and an unimpeachable source of authority to bear the whole burden of responsibility. It is not easy to be free. But such limitations of freedom show not wisdom, but immaturity. They show a people who have not come into their majority as heirs of God's good gifts (see Galatians 3:23-29). Nevertheless, to seek freedom for its own sake is to lose it. Freedom is not for self-indulgence or self-aggrandizement but to serve and love God, in whom alone is found true freedom.

The Covenant Church cherishes this freedom in Christ and recognizes, as one of our forebears put it, that freedom is a gift and the last of all gifts to mature. In the meantime there will be questions and conflicts. Full maturity and full understanding await the day when "the kingdoms of this world become the kingdom of our God and of his Christ, when he shall reign forever and ever" (Revelation 11:15). In the meantime we offer freedom to one another since for Covenant people freedom is not something we claim for ourselves, but offer to the other. In this we are simply sharing the gift of freedom God has given us in Jesus Christ.

7

THEOLOGICAL REFLECTION

In his book *No Wonder They Call Him Savior,* Max Lucado tells the story of the ultimate prank: a group of mischievous youth breaks into the local department store, steal nothing, but switch all the price tags. They cover up their tracks and leave. The amazing thing was that on the next day, for four hours, no one realized that the values had been swapped. Some customers walked away with the best deals and others got swindled. The point of the story is: we live in a world of switched price tags. Things that are truly valuable—honesty, integrity, purity—are sold far too cheaply, and things that are not important at all from an eternal perspective—the nice office window, the Ferrari and the image it promotes, a luxurious lifestyle—are bought at the cost of people's souls. Such is the power of sin to completely distort our personal value system (Romans 1:24-32). We are slaves to whatever we value most (2 Peter 2:19).

Freedom is associated with many things in our culture. Freedom is having plenty of options. Freedom is an indicator of democracy and human will. Freedom is economic choice and the self-made individual. Freedom is liberty and justice for all, culminating in the dream of success and happiness. Freedom is whatever we want it to be!

Ironically, people think that the pursuit of what one wants—no matter how cheap the thrill or perverse the pleasure—is an expression of freedom. But the Bible identifies this kind of moral autonomy as slavery to sin (Genesis 3:5-6; Romans 7:7-20). Here is the paradox of biblical freedom: we are most enslaved when we do what we wrongly desire, and we are most free when we become enslaved to God and do what God rightly wills. The Apostle Paul puts it this way: "When you were freed from righteousness, you were slaves to sin" (Romans 6:20), "but having been freed from sin, you became slaves to righteousness" (Romans 6:18).[1] In other words, false freedom is following our heart's desire when that very same heart is corrupt, twisted, and controlled by wrong values. Sometimes we do not even know where our personal rules for living originate, but like dust of the street we pick up ideas and lifelong habits from unknown worldly sources. As long as we believe in them, they have power over us (Colossians 2:8).

True freedom is letting the One who knows us best—our Creator and heavenly Father (Psalm 139:13-16)—tell us who we are and how to flourish. If, as Genesis says, we truly believe that humans are created for good, then behind the notions of choice, success, participation, liberty, and happiness is the idea that we ought to live as God intended us to live—namely, in pursuit of the good, of God's justice, and of a holy life that points to our Maker.

True freedom is letting our Redeemer and Savior switch the price tags in our moral value system back to their rightful place

The Reality of Freedom in Christ

(Romans 12:1-2). The cross of Jesus liberates us from the reign of sin and death (Galatians 3:13-14; 4:3-7; Romans 6:22-23). The power of Christian freedom is not granted by human laws, rights, privileges, or capital. It is granted by one simple, ongoing event—redemption. Christ has died on the cross to free us from sin, Christ is risen from the dead to free us for new life in him, and Christ will come again to free us, finally, in the fullness of the new heavens and new earth.

True freedom, then, is living in the light of our Lord. It is the power to do good and to live well, or righteously, before God (Romans 6:16-23) who created and redeemed us. In discussing what the Covenant means by affirming the reality of freedom in Christ, we move between God's work of creation and redemption as the poles that define the power of our freedom. Based on God's promises for the church, we offer an alternative to understandings of freedom as toleration, agreeing to disagree, holding any theological position one wishes, and the notion that anything goes. Toleration and agreeing to disagree might be helpful frameworks for living together peacefully, and perhaps are good first steps. However, Christian freedom derives power from God's creating and redeeming work, as promised in Scripture, and calls us into deeper communion than the goal of tolerance affords. This, we believe, is how the Covenant has historically appropriated the affirmation of freedom in Christ.

THEOLOGICAL ROOTS

In 1963, the Covenant Board of Ministerial Standing appointed a committee to prepare a study on the nature of what they called "our highly cherished freedom in the Covenant."[2] The committee was charged with examining the nature and scope of freedom as a unique aspect of Covenant heritage and in its theological and biblical dimensions. The document "Biblical Authority and Christian Freedom," which was developed from the committee's work, is theologically inspiring and forward looking in its contours.

It begins by articulating Christian freedom as becoming what one is meant to be and living out the very purpose for which one is created. Further, it conceives freedom as the state of being free and the process of becoming free.[3] The words *state of being* and *process of becoming* imply that freedom is a gift that is once given and a gift that shapes and transforms us in an ongoing way. Moreover, the words *state* and *process* plunge us deeply into the reality of creation and redemption as they frame freedom. When we refer to freedom as a state of being free, we speak, in part, of our nature as creatures. God designed human beings with a purpose. God blessed creation (Genesis 1–2), each according to its own kind, and proclaimed all of it good! When God blessed Adam, Adam was not only a recipient of God's goodness but also a being endowed with freedom—a being who acts co-creatively with God. This initial freedom is contained within the context of blessing, and in this way represents God's offering of freedom as part of our very nature, hence freedom is a "state." This state of being, as creatures endowed with freedom, is not a static reality, however. It has a *telos*, a purpose. We are free to live into God's designs for God's creatures, and this freedom begs questions. Who are we? How should we live? Who should we become?

In asking ourselves such questions, we shift into the aspect of freedom that is part of our becoming. Genesis 1–3 accounts for these aspects in terms of who we are created to be, namely human beings in the image of God. We are created to reflect, or point to, God. Broadly speaking, becoming free is living in obedience to God's will as given to us in Scripture. In reading God's word and allowing it to penetrate our hearts, we believe that our will conforms to God's will and, further, that this is essential to the process of becoming free to live in Christ.

In a treatise called *On Christian Freedom*, Martin Luther offers insight into conforming to God's will using the doctrines of justification—the doctrine that addresses Christ's death and resurrection as a saving event—and sanctification—the doctrine that addresses our ongoing response to that reality and the transforming work of the Holy Spirit in the lives of believers. He begins the treatise with this dialectic:

- A Christian is a perfectly free lord of all, subject to none.
- A Christian is a perfectly dutiful servant of all, subject to all.

The first statement addresses our freedom from sin. Because Christ died on the cross once and for all, we are bound to our sin no longer. Christ has taken on sin and death, freeing us to live in the light of the resurrection. The second statement refers to our new life in Christ as we are bound to one another through Christ's resurrection. Because Christ has freed us from our sin, we are free for something, namely the wonderful gift of extending love to one another by serving one another.

Just as the Covenant has affirmed freedom's internal partnership between "state" (extended in creation and solidified in the justifying work of Christ on the cross) and "process" (becoming free to live into our new creatureliness), Luther's dialectic reveals the partnership between God's redemptive work and the ethical life, as redemption meets creation in an ongoing way. This partnership gives us the parameters within which to answer the questions of whose we are, how we should live, and who we strive to become. As Paul writes in 1 Corinthians, "For though I am free with respect to all, I have made myself a slave to all" (9:19). And in Romans, he writes that we owe no one anything, except to love one another (13:8). The freedom that Paul denotes is both a state resulting from God's gifting and a process as our response to that gift.

The forerunners of the Covenant, the Lutheran Pietists, understood this dialectic well, both as they engaged in theological reflection and as they practiced their faith. They saw the task of Christian formation to be based on the freedom to choose the gospel. Such freedom cultivated what they—retrieving Luther—described as a living, vital faith or a faith that nests in the heart. Free from sin and free for serving one another in love was more than a theologically rich doctrine—Christian freedom is the basis for a faith that cherishes the reading of Scripture, new life in Christ, the mission of the church, the fellowship of believers, and the inspiration of the Holy Spirit. Freedom, then, is a discipline that embraces our creatureliness in the context of God's justification and co-operative sanctification.

When the Covenant reflects theologically on Christian freedom in the affirmations, the threads of Luther and Pietism are present, and the focus lies on what unites followers of Jesus Christ. We cherish freedom as a gift of God to all willing to receive it, and in this way, we rest first on God's action in Jesus Christ and the gifting of God in creation, and then secondarily on our being willing to receive it. This in itself is freeing, for the reality of freedom is, like God's other good gifts of word, church, and sacraments, initiated by and dependent upon God.

Rightfully, the Covenant frames the sixth affirmation of Christian freedom in terms of practices—receiving the gift of salvation, loving God, and serving our neighbors. This is an essential aspect of how the Covenant understands Christian freedom. Freedom is also, however, framed by our common Christian affirmations and the preceding affirmations. Freedom emerges in the context of the common Christian affirmations that mark us as an apostolic church, a catholic church, a Reformation church, and an evangelical church. These marks establish theological borders and conversation partners that we acknowledge as we live out our freedom in Christ. The voice of the historical church, then, plays a critical role in how we reflect on and practice our faith. Furthermore, we note that the affirmation of the reality of freedom in Christ comes at the end of a list of other important affirmations: the centrality of God's word, the necessity of new birth, a commitment to the whole mission of the church, the church as a fellowship of believers, and a conscious dependence on the Holy Spirit. These commitments to unity with Christ's church universal and to grounding Christian freedom in the Covenant's other distinctive affirmations constitute the authoritative context within which we receive and respond to the freedom extended to us by Christ.

The authority that structures our freedom—God's word—has as its end the unification of Christ's church. What, however, does that mean in practice? If we claim that as Covenanters, the only requirements for membership are baptism and a confession of faith, then are we free to hold any theological position we choose? We use the language of unity on the level of faith and diversity on the level of theological reflection, but have we found agreement on what constitutes unity on the level of faith? Or, to put it in Luther's language, if freedom is a gift that we receive (free lord, slave to none), how are we to extend freedom to others? We now turn to a discussion of *how* we might interpret Scripture in light of the tension between the essentials (or non-negotiables) and non-essentials (or negotiables) of the faith in the context of serving one another in Christian freedom.

READING THE BIBLE IN CHRISTIAN FREEDOM

Until the day of Jesus's return, freedom is something we fight for in our Christian life and put into practice through spiritual discipline. We get an example of such discipline in the life of Paul. In his letter to the Corinthians, for example, we read how the apostle to the Gentiles—though free by faith and therefore subject to no one else's conscience or judgment (1 Corinthians 10:29)—nevertheless out of love has freely chosen to be a slave of all (9:19). He has become all things to all people so that he might win some into the church through his ministry (9:20-23). Though as their pastoral leader Paul was entitled to receive monetary support from the Corinthian church (9:12; cf. Deuteronomy 25:4), he gladly relinquished his rights as an apostle so that he could present the gospel to them "free of charge" (9:12-18). He refused to receive any form of patronage from the congregation. In the same way, Paul expected the Corinthians to relinquish their right to eat whatever they wanted for the sake of freely loving their weaker brothers and sisters who might stumble over the issue of idol food (1 Corinthians 8:1-13; 10:1–11:1).

The case of meat sacrificed to idols (1 Corinthians 8:1) stands as an excellent example of how the local congregation exercises freedom to interpret Scripture and apply its teachings to a wide variety of culturally contingent situations. Idol food was a hot-button issue in Corinth and arguably for the entire early Christian movement in the first century (Acts 15:28-29; Romans 14:1-5; Revelation 2:14-15, 20-23). There was no place in the Roman Empire that a Christian could travel without entering into some social or religious setting where idol food was served.

In his letter to the Corinthian church, Paul addresses three such possible settings where a believer might encounter idol meat and gives a different set of admonitions for each occasion. In 1 Corinthians 8:1-13 (and 10:23-30), he agrees with some elitist members of the congregation (known as "the Corinthian wise" or "the strong") that "an idol is nothing" (8:4). He agrees with the strong that they have the freedom to eat meat sacrificed in a pagan temple as long as they are doing so in the banquet halls (which is something like the cafeteria in a church building) and *not* before an actual idol in the inner sanctuary as a part of a worship service. In the latter liturgical setting (see 10:1-22), Paul is quite clear that no Christian should eat idol food as part of pagan veneration because "you cannot participate in the table of the Lord and the table of demons" (10:21). There are real demonic and spiritual forces at work in a cultic act of pagan worship, and the believer is urged to flee every form of idolatry (10:14). Citing the folly of the Israelites during their wilderness journey and reflecting upon those Old Testament texts that narrate their apostasy (Exodus 32:7; Numbers 11:4; 21:4-9; 25:1-9), Paul warns against a communion with demons that cause the whole church to stumble.

On the other hand, Paul had no qualms of personal conscience about consuming meat in the banquet halls of pagan temples. Since ancient temples (like modern civic centers) doubled as places of assembly for town meetings, weddings, birthdays, and other festive occasions of a social nature, and since leftover idol meat was cheap, high-quality, and readily available, Paul radically departs from his previous Jewish scruples, arguing: "Now food will not bring us any closer to God. We are no worse if we do not eat it and no better if we do" (1 Corinthians 8:8). He bases his conviction concerning the permissibility of idol food within a non-liturgical context upon the *Shema* ("Hear O Israel...") in Deuteronomy 6:4, which states: "The Lord your God is one" (8:4-6). If God is one, there are no other deities, and idols are nothing. Paul also argues for permissibility based on Jesus's own teachings in Mark 7:15-19 that all foods had been declared clean (cf. 8:8).[4] But then in a new interpretive move, Paul turns to a completely different set of biblical texts (Mark 9:42-50; 10:45) and presents the following thesis: Though he is free to eat idol food at the temple, he will not do so on the basis of love. He surrenders his freedom to eat what he wants so that he is free and blameless to love those who, given their past association and participation in idol worship, might be tempted to return to pagan idolatry if they see other Christian believers eating at a temple (8:10-13). If we can imagine a modern-day group of

The Reality of Freedom in Christ

Christians who decide to give up drinking—not because they feel it is inherently dissolute, but because someone in their small group has a past addiction to alcohol and with it is tied to a system of fallen values that can ruin his or her life upon returning to it—we can then begin to understand why Paul would rather never eat meat again than cause another to stumble (8:13).

The third situation that Paul addresses is the case of idol meat sold in the marketplace (1 Corinthians 10:25-30). It was the habit of pagan priests in the ancient world to sell surplus meat sacrificed to idols in the public square. This meat was often bought by clientele, brought home, and served during a private meal. Here Paul advises the Corinthians to eat without problems of conscience because anything that the earth produces is from the Lord and a part of God's good creation (10:26; cf. Psalm 24:1; 50:12; 89:11). He again claims the freedom to eat all foods (cf. Mark 7:15-19) adds yet another injunction based on the ethic of love. If one's host makes it a point to identify the source of the meat as coming from temple sacrifices (1 Corinthians 10:28), then the believer should abstain from it as part of his or her witness to the unbelieving patron and other guests (10:28-29). Just as Christ came to serve and give his life for the many (Mark 10:45), Paul wants the Corinthians to imitate Christ (1 Corinthians 11:1) by seeking not their own advantage but that of the many (10:33).

In the span of three chapters (1 Corinthians 8–10), Paul gives us an example of interpretive freedom as it is linked to the good of love, the advantage of others, and the idea of freely subjecting ourselves to others. He applies a variety of scriptural texts (e.g., the *Shema* of Deuteronomy 6:4; texts on the goodness of creation in the Psalms; the Penteteuchal accounts of Israel's apostasy in the desert; the rights of an apostle in Deuteronomy 25:4) along with the teachings of Jesus (e.g., all foods declared clean in Mark 7:15-19; warnings against stumbling in Mark 9:42-50; the ransom saying of Mark 10:45) to different cultic and social settings involving the consumption of idol food. The church is free to apply Scripture to specific situations as the Holy Spirit leads. As a community of faith, they have the freedom to decide how to practice a particular biblical principle in the daily grind of their ministry and fellowship. To use a metaphor uttered by Jesus himself, "the keys to heaven and earth" have been given to the church so that however they bind and loose Scripture, their interpretation and application of the biblical text has authority over the life of each member in the congregation (Matthew 16:15-19; 18:15-20).[5]

With this freedom also comes the reality that different local churches might not agree on the specific application of a biblical text. The writer of Revelation, for example, does not have the nuanced ethic toward idol food as Paul does. For John the Seer, any consumption of idol meat is sin no matter what social or cultic setting Christians find themselves (Revelation 2:14, 20). Other, probably Jewish, Christians in the church at Rome went beyond idol food and abstained from any kind of meat. This group practiced an ascetic form of vegetarianism (Romans 14:1-5). Different churches in diverse cultural and historical contexts read, heard, interpreted, and applied Scripture non-competitively to address their unique challenges. While there are certainly non-negotiable Scriptural warrants to which all churches must agree (e.g., the *kerygma* or creed in 1 Corinthians 15:3-7 or the reality of Christ's resurrection and ours in 1 Corinthians 15:12-19), churches are nevertheless free to disagree on the non-essentials of the Christian faith and enjoy a diversity of spiritual practices.

Diversity, however, does not mean anarchy. Christians cannot interpret Scripture haphazardly and whimsically. Paul would not allow bad interpreters of the Jesus traditions at Corinth to justify a position of eating idol food at the expense of stumbling a fellow believer. There are good and bad ways to interpret Scripture. There are good and bad ways to apply Scripture. As long as God does not compromise with sin, nor ignore it, but wants to extinguish it, Christians should not attempt to manipulate Scripture to justify their own appetites or vain pursuits (2 Timothy 2:3-4). We are free to apply Scripture to new situations only because the Spirit guides us through the interpretative process, and because we do it together as a community of faith. The act of reading the Bible is more than a human endeavor. Reading Scripture is a means through which God does something to the readers, transforms his creatures, and mediates his grace. When we ask, "Who should we become?" in large part, the answer lies in the discipline of reading Scripture often and reading Scripture together. As we reflect on God's living and active word (Hebrews 4:12), we can be sure that the Spirit of God will free us to interpret the word and to love one another in unexpected, revolutionary, and concrete ways.

FREEDOM AS A SPIRITUAL DISCIPLINE

So now we ask, in light of the reality of Christian freedom, what is required of us? In an insightful *Covenant Quarterly* article on boundaries and freedom, seminary professor James Bruckner shows that the freedom-boundary dynamic is at the center of human relationships. Further, this center is itself an axis of God's blessing. Bruckner writes, "Human blessing is the fullest when humanity's creative freedom and keeping of established boundaries are joined."[6] Human relationships, as lived within the freedom-boundary dynamic, constitute axes through which God extends God's blessing. If we were to fully embrace this reality as a church, the possibilities for growing more deeply together in Christ are rich. God's blessing through freedom is manifest in right relationship not only with God but also with others. Hence, freedom is something to be lived and practiced in ways that challenge us. We should not simply tolerate our brothers and sisters in Christ. We should not merely settle with agreeing to disagree. We should not tritely, and incorrectly, say, "Anything goes in the Covenant!" The commitment to practicing Christian freedom requires what we might call *church discipline,* both on the part of individuals and on the part of the common priesthood.

The Covenant believes that the individual's faith is personal but not private. We fully affirm, as discussed in the affirmation on new birth, the idea that individuals claim the Christian faith by responding to God's extension of grace through faith. Theologian C. John Weborg uses the language of summons and call to describe the process of accepting one's justification in Christ and cooperating in the ongoing formation by the Holy Spirit.[7] We are summoned by God to engage the gospel personally, and to embrace the good news that Christ died, rose, and will come again. In and through this summons, we are called into the common priesthood. This call takes shape as individuals discern their gifts. All have something to offer by way of serving the ministry of Christ's church, as the affirmation of the church as the fellowship of believers states. An important dimension of responding to God in faith is discerning the nature of one's call within (and with) the body. The practices within this include spiritual disciplines of prayer, reading God's word, and worship—all of which equip the church with the wisdom to discern the role of the member within the larger body. Living out one's call constitutes the vocational aspect of Christian freedom and frees persons to live out the giftedness and calling bestowed to each and all in creation.

Another dimension of practicing Christian freedom is the priestly, or ecclesial, dimension. The sixth affirmation notes that freedom is not something that we claim for ourselves; rather, it is a gift given that we in turn offer to our brothers and sisters. The claim behind the idea of offering freedom to one another is the fundamental shared reality of freedom in Christ. Freedom in Christ *exists,* in other words, only as shared. Even while we have remained a denomination for more than a century, there is no getting around the difficulties inherent in sharing. As one of our forebears put it, the practice of Christian freedom is perhaps the last of all practices to mature.

This is not a hopeful outlook in terms of practicing freedom in our life together. However, Christian freedom is something Covenanters have always cherished, and because it is integral to our identity as a church, we remain committed to it. Moreover, because we understand freedom within God's work of creation and redemption, it has actually been an attestation to our hopeful and positive understanding of human beings. The fact that humans are unique in the sense of summons and call assumes also that humans are diverse. And diversity reminds us that we human beings are finite, our knowledge is imperfect, and we are not complete in ourselves. Our forebears saw these anthropological traits as opportunities for the whole body. Engaged faithfully, finitude, imperfection, and brokenness lead to a deeper dependence on God's promises, to an active engagement with the word, and to a stronger sense of interdependence and mutuality—all of which in turn correct and deepen our common faith.

The diversity in the church can and should reflect the reality of our common faith. Rather than lamenting what could be seen only as human shortcomings, the Covenant has always understood our diversity in ways that rested in the vitality of the Christian faith and life in Christ, particularly as it is practiced in spiritually and theologically forming one another in Christ. Covenant resolutions are a great example of how the Covenant practices its freedom. The process by which we agree on resolutions is varied, however. It always involves the process of the whole church in that the delegates to the Covenant Annual Meeting vote on any resolution that comes to the floor. Resolutions are written by groups, such as the Christian Action Committee or local churches, and the agenda always leaves room for discussion and modification. The process can be difficult, but we are committed to discussion around particular theological and moral questions.

David Nyvall affirmed the tensions of exercising freedom, asserting that the theological formation of local congregations is a communal responsibility that requires, at times, difficult conversations. As we practice our freedom in our diverse theological expressions, he challenged the church not to be silent or passive about our differences but rather to engage them. Part of freedom is speaking about and reflecting on issues that cause conflict in the church. The report "Biblical Authority and Christian Freedom" articulates this well:

> It is our duty to approach the areas of theological tension with courage, brotherly [and sisterly] understanding, and unfailing devotion to Christ and the Scriptures. Passive neutrality simply paralyzes our influence and work....In faithfully seeking to understand the revelation given to us in Christ, we make the faith relevant to our day...and find a deepened sense of our unity in Christ.[8]

Relying on the affirmation that the church is a fellowship of believers, the report also addresses how we are to exercise this freedom:

> This means that we show our brothers and sisters the courtesy of hearing and of seeking to understand both his/her words and their meaning and that we do not judge without the opportunity for the other to state their case. It also means that we exercise care in our words and that we never use disagreement as an opportunity for advancement. It also means that we are free to change our own position.[9]

The "hows" of practicing Christian freedom imply mutuality, respect, and vitality in our life together. We are *free* in our relationships and *becoming free* as we help one another conform more closely to the will of God and enter into deeper communion. Over tolerance and distance, it is for this deeper communion that we as God's people strive. We move toward it not by tolerating one another, but by sitting with one another in our diversity and differences. This means that we not only hear and love one another, but that our hearing and loving take shape, namely the shape of forgiveness and reconciliation. If we truly engage freedom as a spiritual discipline, then we are free to love and be loved not only by God but also by one another. The fruit, in essence, is communion.

CONCLUSION

As with other aspects of our faith, Christian freedom is both a gift and a discipline. God's saving work asks something of us, namely that we might receive Christ's love in ways that form and shape who we are as the people of God. The gift of freedom is hard work because it requires that we engage in ongoing transformation, or sanctification. A key way that we do this is by reading our Bibles. As we saw in Paul's letter to the Corinthians, it was through the careful discernment of the whole of Scripture that Paul was able to offer wisdom to the community. Furthermore, in applying the gospel truth that we are to act in love to the advantage of the many, Paul was able to evoke virtue in the life of the Corinthian congregation. Together, identity and discipline constitute what it means to live into freedom as becoming who we were created to be in the light of God's redeeming work. In our personal, ecclesial, and social endeavors, the reality of Christian freedom should shape who we are, who we become, and how we live in both unity and diversity.

Unlike those unknowing shoppers in Max Lucado's story, we have been given a story that tells us what is most valuable. While our world has messed up the price tags, we know that freedom in Christ is priceless, marked not by social, cultural, or political designations but instead by the grace that redeems us from sin and creates us for good. Freedom is not something that we purchase or earn. Freedom is a gift that empowers us to live in faith, hope, and love.

NOTES

1. All English translations of the biblical text are the authors' own.

2. "Biblical Authority and Christian Freedom," Chicago, 1963, 3.

3. Ibid., 9.

4. For further discussion on how Paul applies several Scriptural texts in his ethics on idol food, see Seyoon Kim, "Imitatio Christi (1 Corinthians 11:1): How Paul Imitates Jesus Christ in Dealing with Idol Food (1 Corinthians 8–10)," *Bulletin for Biblical Research* 13.2 (2003), 193–226. A less technical treatment is Richard Hays, *First Corinthians* (Louisville: Westminster John Knox Press, 1997), 134–46; 159–81.

5. For further reading on the binding and loosing of Scripture, see John Howard Yoder, *Body Politics* (Scottdale: Herald, 1992), 1–13.

6. James K. Bruckner, "Boundary and Freedom: Blessings in the Garden of Eden," *The Covenant Quarterly* 57, no. 1 (1999): 15.

7. C. John Weborg, "Pietism: A Question of Meaning and Vocation." *The Covenant Quarterly* 41, no. 3 (1983): 59-71.

8. "Biblical Authority and Christian Freedom," 12.

9. Ibid., 13.

FOR FURTHER READING

"Biblical Authority and Christian Freedom." Evangelical Covenant Church, Chicago, 1963.

Bruckner, James K. "Boundary and Freedom: Blessings in the Garden of Eden." *The Covenant Quarterly* 57, no. 1 (1999): 15-35.

Hays, Richard. *First Corinthians*. Louisville: Westminster John Knox Press, 1997.

Kim, Seyoon. "Imitatio Christi (1 Corinthians 11:1): How Paul Imitates Jesus Christ in Dealing with Idol Food (1 Corinthians 8–10)." *Bulletin for Biblical Research* 13.2 (2003): 193–226.

Luther, Martin. *Freedom of a Christian*. Minneapolis: Fortress Press, 2008.

Volf, Miroslav. *Free of Charge: Giving and Forgiving in a Culture Stripped of Grace*. Grand Rapids: Zondervan, 2005.

Weborg, C. John. "Pietism: A Question of Meaning and Vocation." *The Covenant Quarterly* (Covenant Publications) 41, no. 3 (1983): 59-71.

Yoder, John Howard. *Body Politics*. Scottsdale: Herald, 1992.

For Reflection and Discussion

CHAPTER ONE, COMMON CHRISTIAN AFFIRMATIONS

1) Reflect on your understanding of the word *tradition*. Has this understanding been part of your experience within the church? Has it been beneficial or detrimental in any way?

2) In what ways do you see the Covenant Church being apostolic, or connected throughout history to the early church of the apostles? Read 2 Timothy 3:16 and consider how this relates.

3) In what ways do you see the Covenant Church being catholic, or part of the wider Christian tradition represented in the Apostles' and Nicene Creeds? Reflect on the people who the author said we could claim as belonging to our common tradition. Are there other thinkers or movements that you would claim as being part of our tradition?

For Reflection and Discussion

4) In what ways do you see the Covenant Church being part of the Reformation, the tradition rooted in Luther's turn toward grace? How do you see the effects of Pietism affecting the Covenant Church's theology and practices?

5) In what ways do you see the Covenant Church being evangelical, or shaped by the good news? Consider the author's understanding of this term compared to alternate definitions of the word; how do you and your church understand this term?

6) Consider how your local church reflects, or does not reflect, these particular historic influences on the Covenant Church—apostolic, catholic, Reformation, evangelical. Are there ways that instruction, practices, or prayer related to these four influences might strengthen your worship?

CHAPTER TWO, THE CENTRALITY OF THE WORD OF GOD

1) The author states that the Scriptures are key largely because they introduce us to the living Word, Jesus Christ. How have you seen this in your own life or in your church worship and life together?

2) Look up Isaiah 55:11, 2 Timothy 3:16, and Hebrews 4:12. Consider how these verses explain how the word and the Holy Spirit relate to one another; how is the word alive in an individual's life, in the church, and in the world?

3) How do you see your own identity being shaped by the word? Are there seasons of life when particular theological truths

For Reflection and Discussion

within the word held great importance to you, or times that you've witnessed identity formation in others through the power of the word?

4) As the author writes, "being biblical is not enough," because the Bible can still be used wrongly. Have you witnessed examples of the Bible being used wrongly? How do you think healthy and informed biblical understanding is best cultivated within the church?

5) Have you had experiences of reading Scripture in community where brothers and sisters in Christ interpret or apply biblical truth differently? How has that stretched you or affected your understanding of the Bible?

CHAPTER THREE, THE NECESSITY OF NEW BIRTH

1) How would you define the word *conversion*? How do you define the concept of new birth? How do you relate these definitions to the author's explanation of how Christ's personhood and acts help us to live in Christ?

2) The author states that new birth leads to a new way of living, or discipleship. In your own experience, how do these two realities interrelate or express themselves in your life and in the life of the church?

3) Read Philippians 2:12-13 and reflect on the balance between the role of the Holy Spirit and our own actions on the journey of discipleship. What metaphor or image might be helpful in

For Reflection and Discussion

explaining this balance?

4) Discipleship, or new life, leads to a new community according to this chapter. What characteristics stand out to you as marking this new community? (Draw either from verses already cited or others that come to mind.) In what ways does your church, your community, or your family exhibit these traits, or stand out as living into a new world to those around you? In what ways could this witness become stronger?

5) Reflect on the importance of baptism, including both infant and adult modes, within the Covenant Church. How does your experience with the sacrament of baptism compare to the theological reasoning and promise of new life together found within baptism as described in this chapter?

CHAPTER FOUR, A COMMITMENT TO THE WHOLE MISSION OF THE CHURCH

1) How do you understand the initiating character of God's mission—what is God's role and what is our role when it comes to understanding compassion, mercy, justice, and world mission ministries?

2) Read Luke 10:25-37. How would you summarize this statement of the great commandment for someone else? How would you summarize the Covenant's priority on living out "the whole mission of the church" to someone else?

3) The author connects reconciliation with God and with others

For Reflection and Discussion

together. What relationship do you see between these two realities?

4) Consider the section on "Co-workers with Christ: Relationships and Reconciliation" and reflect on whether or not you've experienced how walking with others, friendship, ethnic diversity, authentic community, and discipleship is part of compassion, mercy, justice, and world missions.

5) What roadblocks or misunderstandings could be present within this affirmation to live out the whole mission of the church? How do Christ's lordship and God's mission influence the sometimes divisive subjects of politics, economics, gender, race, class, and power that are often connected to ministries and advocacy related to this affirmation?

CHAPTER FIVE, THE CHURCH AS A FELLOWSHIP OF BELIEVERS

1) How would the church look or act differently if we believed the statement that the church is "gift before task," that, as the author writes, the church does not depend on our hard work to be God's good church?

2) In what ways have you seen the church sometimes portrayed as resembling just another "voluntary association of individuals" who choose to gather together to form a "we"? What would be the alternate biblical definition of individual and corporate identity within the church?

3) When have you experienced the communal dimension of the

For Reflection and Discussion

fellowship of believers in an especially positive way? Have you experienced the communal dimension the author writes about related to being alive in Christ, or incorporated into Christ's body with others? Or related to walking with God and sharing personal faith and forgiveness with others?

4) Read Galatians 3:23-29 and Ephesians 4:11-16. How do these verses and the chapter point the Covenant Church toward being united and connected as a body? How do these same sources point to relying on diversity or differences among members?

5) How is the Covenant's understanding of interdependence within the priesthood of all believers expressed in your local church? How is it expressed in your experience with the conference or denomination-wide church?

CHAPTER SIX, A CONSCIOUS DEPENDENCE ON THE HOLY SPIRIT

1) What verses, either those listed or those that come to mind, stand out to you as ones that help make the sometimes complexity of the Holy Spirit understandable and clear? How would you describe the Holy Spirit to someone else?

2) Do you have an image of the Holy Spirit, or how the persons of the Trinity interrelate? How does your church portray the Holy Spirit's activity through worship, the arts, or language? How does the dancing metaphor, wind metaphor, or another example from the chapter fit with the images you have experienced?

For Reflection and Discussion

3) Where do you find the Holy Spirit as presence in the church? How is the Holy Spirit expressed in terms of power? Do you think that this presence and power most often elicits a comforting, encouraging, uncertain, or scared response from the church? Why?

4) Drawing from the list of eight clusters of actions (see pages 162-164), reflect on the ways that the Spirit reminds us of who we are, as individuals and as the church.

5) What is the posture of one consciously depending on the Holy Spirit? How does the discussion on fruit and gifts within the chapter help define this answer for you?

CHAPTER SEVEN, THE REALITY OF FREEDOM IN CHRIST

1) True freedom is learning who we are and what we need to flourish from the One who made us, writes the author. How does this compare with common concepts of the term freedom?

2) Do you think it is possible to be subject to none through Christ, and also subject to all? Have you seen this acted out within the church?

3) How is reading the Bible in Christian freedom sometimes acted out in ways that are liberating and constructive? How might this same act be a limiting or destructive practice?

4) In the Christian understanding of freedom, what have we been freed from? What have we been freed for? Are there places within our church that encourage expressing the truths of

For Reflection and Discussion

Christian freedom and practicing how to live with the tension and promise of freedom in Christ as a community?

5) This affirmation purposefully comes at the end of the other five and is built on the realities explored in earlier affirmations. Reflect on how each of the other five affirmations help shape and interact with this last one.

North Park Theological Seminary Faculty

This list of names and titles presents a kind of group portrait of the faculty of North Park Theological Seminary, describing the many and varied roles of its members. It is also a reminder that, while lead writers are identified in the contents, this book is a product of the whole. In committee and all-faculty meetings we conceived the project, then later read and commented on drafts and revisions. We offer it as a natural outgrowth of the teaching we do in seminary and Covenant Orientation classes as well as the preaching and teaching we do in local churches, conference retreats, and denominational gatherings.

Philip J. Anderson, *Professor of Church History*

James K. Bruckner, *Professor of Old Testament*

Richard W. Carlson, *Professor of Ministry, Director of the C. John Weborg Center for Spiritual Direction*

Linda Cannell, *Dean of Academic Life, Professor of Christian Formation*

North Park Theological Seminary Faculty

Mary Chase-Ziolek, *Professor of Health Ministries and Nursing, Director of the Faith and Health Initiative, joint appointment with School of Nursing*

Stephen J. Chester, *Professor of New Testament*

Michelle A. Clifton-Soderstrom, *Associate Professor of Theology and Ethics*

James Dekker, *Associate Professor of Youth Ministry, Co-director of Center for Youth Ministry Studies, joint appointment with North Park University*

Paul H. DeNeui, *Associate Professor of Intercultural Studies and Missiology, Director of the Center for World Christian Studies*

Robert L. Hubbard Jr., *Professor of Old Testament*

Timothy L. Johnson, *Director of Field Education, Associate Professor of Ministry*

Paul E. Koptak, *Paul and Bernice Brandel Professor of Communication and Biblical Interpretation*

D. Brent Laytham, *Professor of Theology and Ethics*

Max J. Lee, *Associate Professor of New Testament*

Carol M. Norén, *Wesley W. Nelson Professor of Homiletics, Director of the Doctor of Ministry in Preaching Program*

John E. Phelan Jr., *Senior Professor of Theological Studies*

Soong-Chan Rah, *Milton B. Engebretson Associate Professor of Church Growth and Evangelism*

Phillis Isabella Sheppard, *Associate Professor of Pastoral Theology*

North Park Theological Seminary Faculty

Klyne R. Snodgrass, *Paul W. Brandel Professor of New Testament Studies*

Norma S. Sutton, *Professor of Theological Bibliography*

Michael Van Horn, *former Associate Professor of Theology and Worship*

Mary C. Miller, *Director of the Making Connections Initiative*